SINCERELY . . .
GIGI

Sincerely...
Gigi

GIGI GRAHAM TCHIVIDJIAN

Daybreak Books

Zondervan Publishing House
Grand Rapids, Michigan

Daybreak Books are published by Zondervan Publishing House, 1415 Lake Drive, S.E., Grand Rapids, Michigan 49506

SINCERELY . . . GIGI
Copyright © 1984 by the Zondervan Corporation
Grand Rapids, Michigan

Library of Congress Cataloging in Publication Data
Tchividjian, Gigi.
    Sincerely—Gigi.
    (Daybreak books)
    1. Christian life—1960– . 2. Tchividjian, Gigi.
I. Title.
BV4501.2.T33   1984   248.4   84-11948
ISBN 0-310-44850-6

Edited by Anne Severance
Designed by Ann Cherryman

All photographs, unless otherwise noted, by Russ Busby.

Printed in the United States of America

84 85 86 87 88 89 / 10 9 8 7 6 5 4 3 2

*T*o all those who, in ways large or small, directly or indirectly, consciously or unconsciously, have encouraged me in my Christian walk by faithfully passing on their knowledge and experience of the Living God and of His Son our Lord Jesus Christ, I sincerely dedicate this book.

CONTENTS

FOREWORD

Gigi is the first of our five children—the mother of seven of our sixteen grandchildren.

It seems but yesterday that she was home—the stubborn, quick-tempered, sensitive, honest, lovable little manager of her younger sisters and brothers.

"*Everyone,* " my wife once laughed, "ought to have at least one Gigi!"

Today we look at her in amazement. An instinctive home-maker, all she has ever wanted to do was to get married, have children, and serve the Lord at the same time—which is exactly what she has been doing for the past twenty years.

When she was only seventeen, God sent the perfect husband for her, Stephan Tchividjian.

During the next ten years they lived in at least twelve different homes in four different countries. From Switzerland to Israel, from a trailer to a gracious home in Florida they moved, and moved again; loving the Lord, loving one another, loving their children, and loving home (for home is an atmosphere rather than a place).

If ever a person was qualified to pass on what she has learned along the way, Gigi is.

She has taught her mother and me much—for which we will be eternally grateful.

—BILLY GRAHAM

Remembering . . .

Remember the days of old, consider the years of many generations: ask thy father, and he will show thee; thy elders, and they will tell thee.
— Deuteronomy 32:7

*T*HE FIRE CRACKLED cheerily in the large fireplace, bathing the living room of my parents' home in a soft, mellow glow. The only other lights were those from the tall Christmas tree which stood by the window, reflecting the snowflakes that were just beginning to fall outside. I sat alone on the brightly polished hearth, hugging my knees and staring into the flames—remembering . . .

This room with its beamed ceiling, its ancient furniture, its loved and worn old brick floor, its chintz-covered couches held so many memories for me. So much of what I knew of the Lord and the Scriptures had been learned right here.

Sundays were special, growing up in this house. Mother woke us with the sound of gospel hymns playing on the record player and the smell of sweet rolls in the oven. After church and lunch, we rested, read, or took long walks to the top of the ridge, passing the "bears' den" on the way, or stopping by the reed field to gather wild flowers. Then, late in the afternoon, my grandparents would arrive to spend the evening.

Our church did not have evening services, so we would eat a quick supper, then light the fire and gather in this room to sing hymns, play Bible games, and share experiences of God's goodness.

With my grandmother at the piano, we sang our favorites— from ancient hymns of the church to the popular new choruses. When our voices gave out, each child cuddled up to an adult who coached as we played "Spit In the Ocean" and "Twenty Questions." One by one, as the children grew sleepy, they were excused and tucked into bed, until only the older ones were left to listen as the adults reminisced.

Daddy might recount an exciting experience of God's faithfulness in his latest crusade, or tell how the Lord had led him in making a difficult decision. My grandfather, a surgeon, might tell how the Lord had touched a patient, bringing not only physical, but spiritual healing. Then a Scripture or specific answer to prayer might be shared. I grew up hearing of God's sovereignty, His constant presence, His protection and mercy, His power and grace, His faithful care and provision of both material and spiritual needs. My parents and grandparents always spoke of the Lord as they would of their best friend. These sessions were not planned, but flowed naturally and spontaneously from hearts filled with love and gratitude.

As I sat on the warm hearth remembering all the happy times experienced around this fireplace, I thought how precious is our Christian heritage and how important to pass it on. I thought of what I wished to share of my own spiritual walk, which has taken me over hills and valleys, into delight and despair, fulfillment and frustration, success and failure. Often, I thought, my weaknesses have outweighed my strengths and, at other times, I have experienced supernatural courage and devotion. As I reflected on my life, I was aware how once again the Lord has used each weakness, each frustration, each failure to bring me into a closer relationship with Himself.

Now, as you participate in this scrapbook of memories, I trust that you will walk with me through the dreary valleys and into the sunshine of mountaintop ecstasies, keeping in mind that it has been during the darker, more difficult moments, when I was at the end of my own strength, that the Lord has chosen to teach me the most valuable lessons. As you read this book, my prayer is that you will be blessed and encouraged in Him.

He Will Take Away
My "Badness"

Being confident of this, that he who began a good work in you will carry it on to completion until the day of Christ Jesus . . . will evermore put his finishing touches to it. — *Philippians 1:6 NIV, Bishop Moule*

I LOVED THE LITTLE ROOM I shared with my sister Anne. It was white, with a lovely bay window where the rhododendron bushes outside snuggled up so close that you could almost reach out and touch their soft pink blossoms. Just beyond, the mountains towered so high that we had to lean way down or go outside to see the top of the ridge we called "Rainbow."

I slept in a big white bed. It really wasn't very big; it was just that I was so small. We had two closets, one on each side of the room. The closet on the right was special, because high above it—out of reach—was a small cupboard where mother would find special treats. (These were confiscated from birthdays and Christmas when we were inundated with toys, and saved for sick-in-bed days.) Once, when I hurt my finger and had to have stitches, mother reached in and found a lovely new baby doll for me.

When I was four, I became quite ill and even the surprise from the hidden cupboard didn't make me feel any better. Mother was concerned and watched me closely. One day she came into my little room and sat down on the edge of the bed. She lovingly stroked my burning forehead and said, "God loves you very much, Gigi—so much that He sent His Son Jesus to die on the cross for you."

Then she repeated once again the story I had heard many times before. She explained how Jesus had been beaten and spit upon and that, although he had done nothing to deserve such treatment, He had taken that cruel punishment for me. He had even been nailed to a cross and left to die, and by taking our sins—our "badness"—on Himself, He was making it possible for us to live with Him forever in heaven when we die. She told me that even if I, Gigi Graham, had been the only little girl in the whole world, God would still have sent His Son to die—just for me.

"Gigi." Mother's voice was very gentle. "If you wish, you could ask Jesus to come into your heart right now."

Oh, how I wanted to do just that! So in simple, childlike faith, I opened my heart to Him and He came in—forgiving my "badness." I certainly didn't understand the theological implications of that moment, nor did I experience much emotionally—but I felt clean and very much loved.

That day long ago, in my little white room, God began something in my life. And He isn't through with me. He continues to shape and mold me, adding His finishing touches.

PASS IT ON . . . Have you personally met Jesus Christ? Are you confident of your relationship with Him?

My mother told me that even if I, Gigi Graham, had been the only little girl in the world, God would have sent His Son to die—just for me.

My Father Loves Me

As a father pitieth his children, so the Lord pitieth them that fear him.
— Psalm 103:13

*T*HE MOUNTAINS OF NORTH CAROLINA offer an ideal setting in which the imagination of an eight-year-old can run wild.

When I was growing up, the woods were full of places for small cowboys and Indians, riding magnificent stick horses and clutching homemade bows, to war with one another. (My "horse" was a palomino with a long, thick mane.) The soft green moss beneath a large oak became the sweeping lawn of an antebellum mansion where my sister and I could use our "dress-up" box and pretend to be grand Southern ladies. Or, if our mood and imagination so dictated, the scene could be transformed into a cozy cabin.

On the hill behind my grandparents' home just next door to ours was a special place we called "Fairyland." It was a secret spot, hidden from view by the thick bushes and undergrowth surrounding the knoll. A carpet of soft, deep emerald moss and several old trees with knotholes of every size and shape provided homes for all the fairies, gnomes, and elves that inhabited this enchanted hideaway. Even the various mushrooms made wonderful tables and chairs just their size. We loved to guess which old knothole housed the "tooth fairy" who faithfully placed a quarter or fifty-cent piece beneath our pillow each time any of us lost a tooth. How he managed to carry such a heavy object was beyond us! One night it rained and his feet got all muddy, for in the morning, there were tiny fairy footprints marching across the bed and pillow. (Mother also had a vivid imagination and artistic ability to match!)

I remember one clear, crisp day when we had been playing up behind our house. A large hollow stump, perched high above the road near a red clay bank, was our fort. We had stocked it with red clay balls (which, more than once, were tossed upon the unsuspecting cars below). On this particular day, I had been playing with friends and had been naughty—a fact that was causing my conscience to hurt badly. The more uncomfortable I became, the harder I played, trying desperately to ignore my conscience. I told myself that what I had done was really not so bad, and that, after all, no one would find out about it. But still I felt miserable.

Suddenly I heard the sound of a car, then commotion in my driveway below. When I heard my daddy's voice, I froze. He had arrived home unexpectedly early. How ashamed I was! I felt cold, then hot. Of all people, I longed to please him. What should I do?

I ran as fast as I could down the hill into the waiting, loving arms of my father, with the assurance that, even if he did find out about my wrongdoing, he would still love me and forgive me.

Since that day so many years ago, I have often suffered from what George MacDonald calls "a conscience doing its duty well, so that it makes the whole house uncomfortable." Though I may try to excuse or cover up my guilt, I am miserable until once again I remember that the only way to find peace is in the strong loving, forgiving arms of my heavenly Father.

PASS IT ON . . . "If we confess our sins, he is faithful and just to forgive us our sins, and to cleanse us from all unrighteousness." (1 John 1:9).

On Display

Let your light so shine before men that they may see your good works, and glorify your Father which is in heaven. — Matthew 5:16

"GIGI! ANNE! BUNNY! FRANKLIN!" they called to the four Graham children. Ned had not yet been born.

It was Sunday afternoon and once again the tourists had arrived. They came by the busload from the nearby conference centers and streamed into our yard, calling our names in the hope that we would come out and pose for pictures. We hid inside behind closed doors and pulled the drapes, peeking out every now and then to watch as they chipped wood from our little rail fence and snapped pictures of our home to take back as souvenirs. As children, we didn't understand all this intrusion and attention. To us, daddy was just daddy. But because he was well-known, we children were on display.

In looking back I realize that this was just another part of God's training program for my life. As Christians, aren't all of us on display before a watching world? We may not always relish the idea; we may find it at times to be inconvenient or burdensome. But we must always be conscious of the fact that representing Jesus Christ to others is a responsibility and privilege reserved for the children of the King.

PASS IT ON . . . May we always be aware that what we *are* speaks so loudly that the world can't hear what we *say*.

The Devil Is A Good Devil

Resist the devil, and he will flee from you. — James 4:7

*T*HE LONG ANTIQUE TABLE was beautifully set with our best silver and china, its highly polished surface reflecting the warm glow of candlelight. It was unusual for us to be gathered in the dining room for our evening meal. We usually ate supper in the cozy kitchen around the big, circular lazy-Susan table in front of the fireplace. (Each of us would hold onto the lazy-Susan and, as soon as the blessing was over, we would see who could be first to spin it. Mother used to say that this prepared us for life in a highly competitive world!) However, since daddy was home from a crusade, we had decided to celebrate his homecoming.

Daddy said the blessing, ignoring the baby who kept interrupting with his "Amen." Then, minding our manners, we passed the Southern fried chicken, homemade rolls, rice and gravy, and, for dessert, Bea's* famous apple pie. How nice it was to be a "complete" family again. How glad we were that daddy was home.

At mealtime fun and laughter always abounded, and during dinner someone began to sing a popular chorus.

> *I've got the joy, joy, joy, joy down in my heart.*
>> *(Where?)*
> *Down in my heart—down in my heart.*
> *I've got the joy, joy, joy, joy down in my heart,*
> *Down in my heart to stay.*

> *I've got the love of Jesus, love of Jesus down in my heart.*
>> *(Where?)*
> *Down in my heart—down in my heart.*
> *I've got the love of Jesus, love of Jesus down in my heart.*
> *Down in my heart to stay.*

---

*Beatrice Long was our faithful housekeeper for over twenty-five years.

Soon, we all joined in and continued through several more verses, concluding with our favorite:

> *And if the Devil doesn't like it, he can sit on a tack.*
> *Sit on a tack—sit on a tack.*
> *And if the Devil doesn't like it, he can sit on a tack.*
> *Sit on a tack to stay.*

To our surprise, daddy looked up with a frown and said a bit sternly, "I don't want you to sing that verse anymore."

We were a bit taken aback, since he was an old softy and tended to spoil us. Turning inquiring eyes on him, we asked why.

"Because," he replied, "the Devil is a good devil."

All of us, including mother, burst out laughing. Then we noticed that he looked very serious.

"What I mean," he explained, "is that the Devil does a very good job of being a devil, and I think it is wrong to take him lightly or mock him. He is real and powerful, and he is no joking matter."

I sat there pondering what daddy had said. I didn't understand fully at the time, but I did begin to develop a healthy respect for Satan and the power he wields. And though I have never been afraid of him, knowing I am under the protection of the blood of Jesus, neither have I given him the satisfaction of being preoccupied with him. Following daddy's advice, I have never touched those things associated with Satan's domain. Years later, when the occult and witchcraft became a popular fad, I asked the Lord to help me to be sensitive and discerning concerning these matters, whether it be a game, and book, or a movie, and have remembered the lesson learned so long ago around the dinner table.

PASS IT ON . . . Never underestimate the power of Satan. The Devil is a "good" devil and does his job effectively and well, so "put on the whole armour of God, that ye may be able to stand the wiles of the devil" (Eph. 6:11).

Good-by Again

This one thing I do, forgetting those things which are behind, and reaching forth unto those things which are before, I press toward the mark. — Philippians 3:13-14

MOTHER STOOD WAITING outside the door. The suitcases were packed and standing in the hallway, ready to be loaded into the car. We children ran around the driveway, laughing and playing while we waited for daddy. Suddenly his tall, handsome figure appeared in the doorway, overcoat slung over one arm, hat on his head. We ran to him, dreading what we knew would be another long separation. He took each of us in his strong arms, holding us tightly, and then he kissed us good-by.

I couldn't bear to look into his eyes, because I knew they would be glistening with tears. Though there were many such good-bys while we were growing up, it never got easier. We backed away and watched as daddy took mother in his arms, kissing her warmly and firmly, knowing it would be some time before he would hold her again.

Then before we knew it, daddy was whisked away in the car, around the curves and down the steep mountain drive. We listened to the retreating sound of the engine and waited for the final "toot" of the horn as he reached the gate. Another plane to catch, another city, another crusade, another period of weeks before we would be together as a family once more.

I turned to look at mother, sensing her feeling of loss and loneliness. Her eyes were bright with unshed tears, but there was a beautiful smile on her face as she said, "Okay, let's clean the attic! Then we'll have LaoNaing and Lao I* up for supper!"

Not once did my mother ever make us feel that by staying behind she was sacrificing her life for us children. By her sweet, positive example, her consistently unselfish spirit, and her total reliance upon the person of Jesus Christ, we were kept from

---

*Chinese for maternal grandmother and maternal grandfather. Mrs. Graham's parents, the Nelson Bells, served for twenty-five years as missionaries to China.

bitterness and resentment. We learned, instead, to look for ways to keep busy and prepare for daddy's homecoming.

Years later, I asked mother how she had endured so many years of good-bys. She laughed then and quoted the old mountain man who said, "Make the least of all that goes, and the most of all that comes."

> We live a time
> secure;
> beloved and loving,
> sure
> it cannot last
> for long,
> then—
> the goodbyes come
> again—again—
> like a small death,
> the closing of a door.
> One learns to live
> with pain.
> One looks ahead,
> not back—
> never back,
> only before.
> And joy will come again—
> warm and secure,
> if only for the now,
> laughing,
> we endure.
> —Ruth Bell Graham*

PASS IT ON . . . Don't regret what is past, but cherish what you have, looking forward to all that is to come and relying on Jesus Christ moment by moment.

---

*From *Sitting By My Laughing Fire* by Ruth Bell Graham, copyright © 1977 by Ruth Bell Graham; used by permission of Word Books, Publisher, Waco, Texas 76796.

The Example

Be thou an example of the believers, in word, in conduct, in love, in spirit, in faith, in purity. Till I come. — 1 Timothy 4:12-13

SPENDING THE NIGHT at my grandparents' house was always a special treat. When I was all ready for bed, I grabbed my pillow and my school clothes, ran up our drive, crossed the little wooden bridge, darted across the street, and down into my grandparents' yard. The back porch light was still on, and I knew the door would not be locked.

When I ran in, LaoNaing not only gave me a hug, but some freshly baked custard and one of her special mints. I kissed her good night, then circled through the living room to find Lao I. After giving him a kiss, I climbed the stairs to bed.

The small sleeping porch was perched high among the trees. With the bed pushed up against the windows, it was almost like being in a tree house. I loved falling asleep in the soft glow of the full moon.

Though I awoke early, the birds were up before me, singing their hearts out—blue jays, cardinals, thrashers, Carolina chickadees, and, every now and then, a bright yellow-and-black Baltimore oriole or a vivid blue indigo bunting. Sometimes even a pileated woodpecker would drill just outside my window, waking me with a start.

The first rays of sunlight were just beginning to touch the ridge behind the house. I lay there watching as they gradually lit the summit, then slowly slid down the mountain. Before I left for school, the sun would have already reached the valley, warming us with its presence.

I could smell breakfast cooking—bacon, eggs, and hot biscuits! I got up and dressed quickly, then tiptoed down the stairs. When I reached the bottom landing, I peered around the corner into the living room. Yes, he was there as he was every morning, on his knees in front of the big rocking chair. I stood watching him until LaoNaing called us to breakfast. He got up slowly, rubbing his eyes before he replaced his glasses, his forehead still red and creased from the impact of his folded hands. He saw me and smiled. Giving me a warm hug and a big kiss, we went into the kitchen together.

I knew that this active surgeon, church layman, writer, former missionary to China, and family man had been up long before dawn, spending time with the Lord. He had an extensive prayer list, and I felt warm and secure, knowing he had already prayed for me. Now he was refreshed and eager to meet the rest of his busy day.

My grandfather never disappointed me as a man or as a Christian. Until the day he died, he set an example of practical, balanced, fun-loving, disciplined, godly living.

When I examine my own life, I wonder what my children see. Do they see a concern for others, or do they see criticism, cynicism, and compromise? Do the things of eternal and spiritual value have priority in my life, or am I too preoccupied with the material and temporal things? Which is more important—my children's little feet or their footprints? The fun we have eating popcorn together, or the salt and butter on the carpet? Do they discern a sense of peace and serenity in our home, or strife and tension? Do I walk my talk? Is there a noticeable difference in my life? Do they perceive acceptance, love, and understanding? Do they experience the results of my prayers? Is the fruit of the Spirit exemplified in my life?

PASS IT ON . . . Lord, "I will try to walk a blameless path, but how I need your help, especially in my own home, where I long to act as I should" (Ps. 101:2 LB).

Am I Going To Heaven?

For by grace are ye saved through faith; and that not of yourselves: it is the gift of God: Not of works, lest any man should boast. — *Ephesians 2:8-9*

ONE FRIDAY AFTERNOON, Mother promised to take Anne, Bunny, and me to our mountain cabin to spend the night.

When we arrived home from school, Mama had everything all packed, and after changing into playclothes, we piled into the Jeep. Soon we were bouncing along the old dirt road that climbed steeply upward to the small one-room cabin.

After a supper of hot dogs and hot chocolate prepared over the open fire, we sat on the porch, reading and talking until dark. Then suddenly I asked a question that had been troubling me all afternoon.

"Mama, if I die, will I go to heaven?"

I had good reason to ask, for that very afternoon, for the umpteenth time, I had been punished for teasing my little sister.

"You tell *me*," was her reply.

"I don't know."

"Want me to tell you how you can know?" asked Mama.

"I don't think you can know for sure."

"Oh, yes, you can."

"How?"

"First," she explained, "you know that you are a sinner, don't you?"

"Of course!" I agreed. There was never any doubt about that!

"Then, you confess your sins to Him."

"I've done that," I nodded. "After I got so mad this afternoon, I told Him I was sorry three times—just in case He didn't hear me the first time."

"He heard you the first time," Mama acknowledged sagely. "You are a child of God because you asked Jesus into your heart. Do you remember being born into God's family when you were only four?"

"No," I shook my head. "I don't remember it. I only know

what you've told me. And I'm still not sure I'm going to heaven."

"Gigi, just because you can't remember the day doesn't make it any less real. Would you call God a liar?" Mama asked sternly.

"Of course not!" I protested.

"But that's just what you're doing," she insisted. "He tells us that if we confess, He will forgive (1 John 1:9). If we believe, we have eternal life (1 John 2:25). You have confessed and you believe, yet you don't think God will keep His promise. That's the same as calling Him a liar." She paused a moment for me to reflect on her words. "Don't you recall what John 3:16 says? Recite it for me."

And I repeated the familiar, much-loved verse: "For God so loved the world, that He gave His only begotten Son that whosoever believeth in Him shall not perish but have everlasting life."

Then Mama held up a piece of paper and said, "Whoever wants it can have it."

I snatched it from her fingers.

"What makes you think I said you?" Mama demanded.

"You said 'whoever,' " I replied.

"Exactly."

We knelt beside the cabin's bed and prayed for assurance.

"Mama," I said breathlessly as we rose to our feet, "I feel like a new person."

The next day, this "new person" scampered down Assembly Drive to the Montreat gate and uprooted a dozen water lilies that had just been planted in time for the arrival of the season's first tourists and conferees. Mama escorted me to the town manager's office with the evidence wilting in my tight little fist, my face pale as I worried aloud that I was going to be thrown into jail (Mama saying absolutely nothing to dispel the fear).

I confessed and apologized. With so much practice, I was a good little "repenter."

That night as Mama tucked me into bed, I asked plaintively, "Have I been good enough today to go to heaven?"

"Now, how much," wrote Mama in her diary that night, "should I impress on Gigi the doctrine of Salvation by Grace when, really, for a child of her disposition, one could be tempted to think that salvation by works would be more effective?"

That was not the last time I was plagued with doubts, because "being good" has been harder for me than for some. The Devil loves to make me feel unworthy of God's love and grace to the point that I even wonder at times if I am really saved.

But I am grateful the Scriptures teach that His love is unconditional, and that salvation is by grace alone, not dependent on my performance or feelings.

PASS IT ON . . . Beware! Often our feelings can be Satan's counterfeit for faith.*

*Adapted from pp. 141–42 in *A Time for Remembering: The Ruth Graham Story* by Patricia Daniels Cornwell. Copyright © 1983 by Patricia Daniels Cornwell. Copyright © 1983 by Ruth Bell Graham. By permission of Harper & Row, Publishers, Inc.

But How? How? How?

I am the vine, and ye are the branches: He that abideth in me, and I in him, the same bringeth forth much fruit: for without me you can do nothing. — *John 15:5*

I COULD SEE THE FIRST rays of light as the sun made its way slowly up Little Piney Ridge. Only a few more minutes and it would burst forth, ushering in another day. Until then, I would sit at my window and savor these quiet moments.

The early morning fog still covered most of the sleepy valley below, obscuring the little town of Black Mountain that was just beginning to stir. But the tops of the Blue Ridge Mountains stood out dark and clear against the dawn. And just beneath my window, the lilac bush was heavy with dew, its large fragrant blossoms bowed with the weight, poised in anticipation of a new day. And it promised to be a glorious one!

I prayed fervently, *O Lord, please let this be the day You and I get it together!*

After reading a portion of my Bible, I prayed again, giving the Lord my day. I felt so good and it was all so beautiful. Surely I wouldn't blow it today. Then I bounded down the stairs in the direction of the heavenly aroma of bacon and eggs coming from the kitchen.

Well, I tried. I really did. But I didn't make it all the way through breakfast. First I argued with one of my sisters, then sassed my mother when she scolded me. And when I realized what I had done, I became so discouraged that I just gave up on that day completely.

And so goes the story of my life—trying to be good. I am a struggler. If only I could arrive at this or that spiritual plateau, or if only I could eliminate this or that problem or weakness, then I would be worthy. Living the Christlike life just hasn't come easily for me. But the deep longing and desire to be like Him started in my childhood, continued into my teens, and followed me into marriage.

Several years later I was sitting at another window overlooking another valley. By this time I was married to Stephan and living in Switzerland. I had been reading one of the many books on "victorious Christian living" that now filled my shelves. And as I gazed out over the flower-strewn fields to the snow-covered Alps beyond, I suddenly found tears streaming down my cheeks, and I cried out in utter frustration, "But Lord! How? How? How?"

As I sat there with my bowed head in my hands, I remembered something I had read some years before: "His Father said, 'Leave that book and read the Book that thou lovest best. Thou wilt find it much simpler.' "

Perhaps I had been reading too many books, trying too hard. My heavenly Father then reminded me that I was created not to *be*, but to *belong*. For a moment I reveled in that thought. Not to be always positive, always smiling, always "up" as the books intimated—but to rest in Him and in His Word alone? It seemed too good to be true! But it was and is true. Our part is to focus on belonging, abiding, and He will take care of the rest.

PASS IT ON . . . "We need to quit struggling and start snuggling." —Corrie Ten Boom

I Remember A Day In September

I the Lord do keep [her]; I will water [her] every moment; lest any hurt [her], I will keep [her] night and day. — Isaiah 27:3

*T*HE SUFFOCATING SEPTEMBER HEAT and humidity of central Florida greeted me as I climbed from the car. Sand immediately filled my shoes, and gnats swarmed around my face. But as I looked around at the enchanting sight, the discomfort was all but forgotten. I had never seen anything quite so lovely.

The old Spanish estate was set in the midst of four hundred acres of semitropical gardens and orange groves. Huge oak trees laden with Spanish moss lent an almost exotic flavor. The large red-tiled mansion was graced by courtyards, formal gardens, fish ponds, colonnades, and a sweeping lawn that fell gently into the quiet lake.

I strolled around the grounds, trying to acclimate myself. It was like walking through one of the popular romantic novels girls of my age so loved to read. My emotions were mixed. I had wanted to come here, but beautiful as it was, it was not the setting for a romantic novel, nor was I the heroine of a make-believe plot. This was real, and the reality of it sent a strange feeling rushing to the pit of my stomach. In just a few minutes my family would climb back into the car, leaving me here alone. And with the exception of Christmas and summer vacations, this lovely, strange, unfamiliar place would be "home" for the next four years of my life. Not yet thirteen years old, I was going to boarding school for the first time.

My trunks and suitcases were carried to my room, introductions were made, good-bys said, tears shed. Then my family left, taking with them all of my courage, self-confidence, and joy, and leaving me with a terrible sense of loneliness and a horrible pain called homesickness.

Thus began my first period of true testing. It was time to put into practice everything I had learned up to this point. Now was the time to try God, to prove Him true to His promises, to place my total trust and confidence in Him alone, to learn to cast all my anxieties upon Him. Now was the time to discover the reality of His presence; to find out for myself that He really did care about me, Gigi, as an individual; to rest in the truth that I was His personal concern and that nothing is too big or too small to escape His notice.

That was many years ago, but the lessons I absorbed in those four years have never been forgotten. The Lord Jesus became my Best Friend. I learned to rely on Him and to this day He has never once failed me nor disappointed me.

PASS IT ON . . . When we are in a situation where Jesus is all we have, we soon discover that He is all we really need.

Most Important Of All

He that is faithful in that which is least is faithful also in much.
— Luke 16:10

*I*T WAS ONE OF THOSE DELIGHTFULLY balmy days so typical of Florida. The doors of the classroom were open, allowing the soft breezes to blow the fragrance of orange blossoms through the room. I had arrived early and was sitting quietly at my desk, savoring the sensations of early spring. One by one the other students filed in and suddenly the shrill school bell sounded, interrupting my reverie and indicating the beginning of another school day.

The teacher, as she did each day, commenced the hour with a brief devotional. I must admit I was distracted by the singing of the birds, the warm breezes, and the sweet aromas, and I found it hard to concentrate—until something she said caught my attention.

"The only thing the Lord requires of us," she was saying in conclusion, "is faithfulness."

Both excitement and peace flooded me at those words. There, sitting at my school desk in central Florida, a big burden was lifted from my shoulders. Because, you see, even at my tender age, I had been feeling an awesome responsibility to measure up. There was so much to live up to, so many big footsteps to walk in, so many examples to follow that I just didn't see how I was going to do it!

But—if the Lord's only requirement of me was faithfulness, then *He didn't expect me to be like anyone else!* And if the importance was in the faithfulness and not in the "greatness" of the task, then with His help I could serve and please Him in my own unique way. What a comfort! From that day on, my prayer was that no matter what He gave me to do—whether great or small, public or private—I would be faithful.

For me, faithfulness has meant staying up all night with a sick child, ironing my husband's suits when he forgets to take them to the cleaner's, washing windows, pulling weeds. For others, it may mean remaining in a mundane or monotonous job or in a behind-the-scenes ministry.

Not everyone possesses boundless energy or a conspicuous talent. We are not equally blessed with great intellect or physical beauty or emotional strength. But we have all been given the same ability to be faithful. And, as we are told in the parable of the talents, it is the faithfulness that receives the commendation of God: "Well done, thou good and faithful servant: thou hast been faithful over a few things, I will make thee ruler over many things" (Matt. 25:21).

More than twenty years have passed since my teacher shared this simple truth with us, but it continues to be a source of encouragement to me even now. I still tend to compare myself to others and, sometimes, when I see those gifted Christians who seem to achieve so much for the Lord, I am tempted to admonish myself: "Gigi, if they can do it, so can you! After all, look at the advantages you have had!" Then I recall that balmy day so long ago and hear Him saying to me: "I am not requiring all this of you. You have placed these pressures and expectations on yourself. I ask only that you be faithful."

PASS IT ON . . . The Lord doesn't expect greatness or perfection from us, only faithfulness. Even the simplest soul can fulfill that requirement.

The Same Spirit Says
The Same Thing

Trust in the Lord with all thine heart; and lean not unto thine own understanding. In all thy ways acknowledge him, and he shall direct thy paths. — Proverbs 3:5-6

*D*ADDY HELD MY HAND EVER SO TIGHTLY as we climbed the steep, winding road to the little church that clung to the side of the mountain overlooking Montreux, Switzerland.

The jonquils nodded their heads approvingly as we passed, and the yellow blossoms of the forsythia seemed to have opened overnight just for us. The day had been overcast with a drizzle of fine mist, but as we pulled up to the church, the sun burst forth in celebration. Daddy gave me one last, reassuring squeeze. We stepped into the church and into a new life for me. It was my wedding day.

As the soloist sang "Oh, Perfect Love," my thoughts wandered to another mountain setting, only six months before. . . .

I was sitting on the window seat in my bedroom overlooking the Blue Ridge Mountains. The trees were bare and the air so crisp and clear that I could distinctly see all the activity in the valley below. Bright Christmas lights enticing shoppers. Cars winding slowly up the narrow mountain roads. Yellow-and-black school buses, stopping to unload children who were hurrying home to warmth and supper. And, every now and then, a long freight train inching its way lazily across the valley floor. Although I took note of all these familiar sights, my mind was thousands of miles away—high in the Swiss Alps.

In my lap was a letter from a handsome, godly man, six years my senior, who was asking me to marry him and move to Europe. Although I had met him several years earlier, I didn't know him well nor had we had any contact for many months. Yet, somehow, I knew the Lord was directly involved in this proposal. I glanced down and my eyes fell again on the sentence that kept turning over and over in my heart. It read simply: "The same Spirit says the same thing."

As I watched the late afternoon sun slide slowly behind the ridge, I wondered how a naïve, seventeen-year-old girl could make such a momentous decision. I got up and walked to the bedside table where my Bible lay open to Isaiah 1:19: "If ye be willing and obedient, ye shall eat the good of the land."

Was I willing? Did I really want God's will more than anything else in my life? Was I willing to be available to Him, to trust Him, to obey Him? Was I willing to follow His leading even if it meant leaving all that was dear and familiar to me and giving myself to a man I didn't yet know well enough to love?

I knew that I had to be able to answer these questions before I could know God's perfect plan for my life.

The days passed, and I continued to search my Bible and my heart. Then one day, I awoke with a real sense of joy. I knew beyond a shadow of doubt that I could answer a resounding YES to each of those probing questions. Yes, I did want His will more than anything. Yes, I would follow and obey Him. Yes, I could trust Him. Hadn't He said, "For I know the plans I have for you . . . plans to prosper you and not to harm you, plans to give you hope and a future"? (Jer. 29:11 NIV).

The peace "that passeth understanding" flooded my being that December day, and I knew that the same Spirit that had impressed dear Stephan to ask me to marry him was now assuring me, by faith and not by feeling, to answer yes. . .

My thoughts were suddenly brought back to the present moment by the majestic chords of the "Wedding March." I clutched daddy's arm tightly as we walked down the aisle of that picturesque church. I heard him say, "Her mother and I do" as he answered the question "Who gives this woman to be married to this man?" and then I was exchanging rings with my new husband—rings in which were inscribed the words: "The same Spirit says the same thing."

PASS IT ON . . . When we let go and let God have His way in our lives, we will never be disappointed because "as for God, his way is perfect" (2 Sam. 22:31).

It Mattered Less Than Love

*And be ye kind one to another, tenderhearted, forgiving one another,
even as God, for Christ's sake, hath forgiven you.* — *Ephesians 4:32*

ONE DAY WHILE DISCUSSING the subject of love, I asked
my children for their definition of marriage. One of my little
boys piped up and said, "It's when you find someone you want
to keep!"

Stephan and I entered marriage with the firm conviction that
it would be a lifelong commitment—not just a convenience
held together by a contract. We began our union on a solid
foundation of shared faith, love, and a mutual desire to glorify
God. But that doesn't mean it has always been easy or smooth.
We have had our share of struggle and conflict.

Stephan is from an Armenian-European background, and I,
from a small Southern town in the United States. We were
married in Switzerland and made our first home in one of its
lovely valleys—very romantic, especially when the full moon
would slide up from behind the mountains. But even this fairy-
tale setting could not ease the adjustments between two such
different persons.

There were many cultural shocks and hurdles to overcome. I
didn't speak a word of French at the time, and with family and
friends thousands of miles away, it wasn't long before I became
lonely and homesick.

I discovered early in our marriage that the honeymoon high
was not destined to be a steady marital experience, but that
reality demanded the unique blending of two distinct individuals from widely differing backgrounds and contrasting cultures.
Difficulties were sure to arise; misunderstandings would become full-blown arguments; feelings would be hurt. But with
each disagreement I found myself more determined than ever
to develop, to deepen, to strengthen and to encourage our love
and commitment to each other.

Someone has said that true marriage is not without conflict,
but is ever reconciling its conflict. This will mean determina-
tion, understanding, seeing things from the other's point of
view, humility, being willing to be the first to say "I'm sorry."

Twenty years, seven children, and many arguments later, I can assure you that it's worth it!

> I do not say that there were no
> Misunderstandings, discontents,
> And hurts. I would it had been so.
> Strange how the heart sometimes assents
> To angers that the will asserts.
> But these we learned to live above.
> I do not say there were no hurts.
> I say they mattered less than love.
> —Jane Merchant*

PASS IT ON . . . Don't expect from your mate what only Jesus Christ can give.

*From *Halfway Up the Sky* by Jane Merchant. Copyright © 1957 by Abingdon Press. Used by permission.

Confined

O God of my righteousness: thou has enlarged me when I was in distress. — *Psalm 4:1*

THE ICY WIND BURNED MY CHEEKS, but I stood there as long as I could, watching the retreating figure of the man I loved as he trudged off into the snow to catch his train. I turned to close the door and, suddenly, loneliness engulfed me.

Stephan had been called away for a few weeks of military duty, and I was left with only two infant children for company in this small German-speaking village high in the Swiss Alps, miles away from our own home. Tears stung my eyes as I turned out the lights, gathered the children, and climbed the stairs to bed.

If the nights were long, the days seemed interminable. Each morning I awoke with the same sinking feeling. After breakfast I would bundle up the children and walk to the village that lay a mile down the winding road. We would buy our groceries, window-shop, occasionally stop at a tearoom for hot chocolate, then walk home. But each time I entered the old chalet, I felt its unfamiliar walls closing in on me.

I felt abandoned and confined—confined to a small apartment that was cold and foreign, confined by the walls of snow outside the windows, confined by the language barrier, confined by the fact that my family and friends were far away, confined by the small children who couldn't understand my frustration. I felt pressed on every side, and it wasn't long before self-pity began to work her way into my very being, and I was utterly miserable.

One day as I sat alone at the kitchen table fussing at the Lord, it occurred to me that I was missing a perfect opportunity to practice the presence of God and prove His promises. So each afternoon after the children were tucked into bed for their naps, I would stoke the fire, fix a pot of tea, sit down at the antique desk, and spend time with the Lord. I cried out to Him like Isaiah when he said, "O Lord, I am oppressed; undertake for me" (38:14). And, like David, I poured out my frustration: "My spirit is overwhelmed within me; my heart within me is desolate" (Ps. 143:4). Then I would steep myself in His Word, soaking it in, allowing Him to love me.

Oh, how real He became to me! True to every promise, He took my burden, lifted me up, undertook for me, and gave me peace and joy in the midst of my loneliness. Soon I was able to enjoy the walks to the village, appreciate the companionship of my children, enjoy the beauty around me—the snow glistening in the sunlight, the glory of the mountain peaks, the skaters and skiers in their bright jackets. And, before I knew it, it was time to throw open the door and greet Stephan once again.

Many years have come and gone since that cold, lonely winter. And in looking back, I wouldn't trade that experience for anything. The misery lasted only a few weeks, but the precious lesson has lasted a lifetime.

My experience was not unique. Everyone has times when they feel confined—by small children, finances, illness, loneliness, circumstances beyond control. But I have discovered:

> If loving hearts were never lonely,
>   If all they wish might
>   always be
> accepting what they look for only,
>   They might be glad,
>   but not in Thee.
>   —A. L. Waring

PASS IT ON . . . When times are difficult and circumstances trying, may we remember to practice the presence and prove the promises of God.

He Is Coming!

Looking for that blessed hope, and the glorious appearing of the great God and our Saviour Jesus Christ. — Titus 2:13

"MAMA, COME QUICK! Come quick!" my young son called excitedly, the cold winter air rushing past the small snow-suited frame silhouetted in the open doorway.

I ran to see what he wanted. He grabbed my hand and pulled me into the fresh snow that was just beginning to melt in the warm sunshine.

"There! There! Up in the sky!" he cried, pointing to a bright object. With anticipation in his blue eyes and hope in his voice, he asked, "Mama, is that Jesus coming back?"

Oh, how I wished that I could have shouted a resounding yes. Instead, I took the little fellow in my arms and explained that it was just an airplane reflecting the afternoon sun. Together we watched as the plane continued its flight across the sky and over the mountain peaks.

As I rearranged his cap and adjusted his mittens, I sensed a gentle rebuke in his disappointed face. I remembered how I, too, had thrilled to the thought of the imminent return of the Lord Jesus. But I had become so caught up with the business of everyday living that I had lost my awareness of the reality that He could come back at any time.

The Scriptures teach that there is a special crown—a crown of righteousness—set aside for those who look forward to and love His appearing. (See 2 Tim. 4:8.) Will He find me waiting, watching, ready?

* * *

It was Easter—my favorite time of year. I was visiting my grandmother and grandfather Graham in Charlotte, North Carolina, and woke up on Easter Sunday to the horrible realization that my mother had forgotten to pack a Sunday dress—much less a special one! I did the best I could. I wore an aqua skirt and a navy blue sweater that didn't match, and when we arrived at church, there I was—the ugly duckling in the midst of all those beautiful Southern ladies and their daughters, dressed in their very finest. I will never forget the terrible feeling of being so unsuitably dressed for that special occasion.

When the Lord returns, will we be awkwardly attired in our good works which are like filthy rags in His eyes? (See Isa. 64:6.) Will we be wearing the old hand-me-downs of our parents and grandparents? Or the latest religious fashion? Or will He find us appropriately clothed in His righteousness alone?

"I will greatly rejoice in the Lord, my soul shall be joyful in my God; for he hath clothed me with the garments of salvation, he hath covered me with the robe of righteousness" (Isa. 61:10).

* * *

When I was a child, daddy and mother would often take the train from our small town in North Carolina to Washington, D.C., or New York. My sisters and I loved seeing them off at the train station and meeting them when they returned home. I can still feel the surge of excitement when I heard the whistle blow and knew that the large locomotive was just around the last curve. Any minute now and I would see its big, bright light, and then I would be in my parents' arms again! But if I had been naughty while they were away, I felt self-conscious and embarrassed, knowing that a bad report of my behavior would bring them disappointment. Then I experienced not joy, but shame.

So it is with our Lord's return. Will He find us eagerly waiting, or will we be ashamed to see Him? "And now, little children, abide in him; that, when he shall appear, we may have confidence, and not be ashamed before him at his coming" (1 John 2:28).

PASS IT ON . . . May the expectation of His coming not only bring joy and comfort to our hearts, but may this realization also purify our lives so that we will be ready . . . whenever . . .

Look Up

When I am afraid, I will trust in thee. — *Psalm 56:3*

STEPHAN, THE CHILDREN AND I slowly climbed the steep, narrow road that wound its way up the side of the mountain to our little village high in the Swiss Alps. The sun was sinking lower and lower behind the ridge that loomed up just ahead, and we knew it would be only a few more sharp turns before we would be face-to-face with the dreaded bridge. As dusk fell, the large evergreen trees seemed to close in on us, casting ghostly shadows along the road. We never liked crossing the rickety old bridge, especially since caution signs had been posted. But it was the only way to span the deep ravine that separated one side of the valley from the other.

There it was—challenging and taunting us. As we started across, grateful that no other cars were adding their weight, our four-year-old son suddenly cried out in fear. His younger sister looked at him with understanding. Perhaps reassuring herself as much as her brother, she said, "Stephan-Nelson, don't be afraid. Look up—not down."

There have been many times in my own life when I have been afraid. Afraid of the unknown, afraid when a child has been very ill, afraid when the plane tossed unmercifully during a stormy flight, afraid to speak out, afraid that I might disappoint or be disappointed, afraid of being found out, afraid of rejection, afraid to take a stand, afraid of losing, afraid to be alone, afraid to make a decision, afraid of pain.

Some of my fears are real; some of them are imaginary. Some are physical; others, psychological or emotional. Some are for myself and some are for loved ones. Whatever the fear, it is keenly felt—an unpleasant experience. And, invariably, the bridge between despair and hope looks awesome and precarious when I am looking down at myself—my circumstances, my feelings, my emotions—instead of looking up and trusting in Him whom my soul loves.

*Turn your eyes upon Jesus
Look full in His wonderful face;
And the things of earth will grow strangely dim
In the light of His glory and grace.**

PASS IT ON . . . We are lifted above our circumstances when we look into the face of Jesus.

Remember to look up, not down.

Above The Fog

I lift up mine eyes to the hills. Where does my help come from? My help comes from the Lord. — Psalm 121:1, 2 NIV

IT WAS A COLD, DREARY, foggy day in our little Swiss village. Tired of being indoors, the children begged to go for a ride in the *telecabine* which ran up to one of the mountain peaks directly behind our chalet. I had to admit that it sounded tempting, so leaving the household chores behind, I bundled the little ones in their warm coats and soon we were all snuggled into the tiny cable car.

In only a matter of moments we were suspended high above the ground, moving slowly through the dense fog that engulfed us. All of a sudden we broke through the clouds and there, surrounding us, bathed in brilliant sunshine, were the glorious mountain peaks. We stepped out of the little car and onto the terrace where we sat in the sun, soaking up its warmth while we sipped hot chocolate and tried to capture forever the splendor of the moment.

All too soon it was time to return. We descended slowly, and it wasn't long before we were once again enshrouded by the low-hanging clouds and the dreary dampness of the valley fog.

I couldn't help realizing that this experience is often paralleled in my life. I love the mountaintop experiences, the times when I am transported beyond the fog to bask in the warmth of the Son and His love, leaving the dailiness and dreariness behind and feeling only the splendor and majesty of His presence. But often I feel confined to a life of foggy valleys— the mundane, the frustrations, the difficulties of valley life that seem to overwhelm me, and I grow weary of trying to climb out of the fog.

> *The hills on which I need to gaze*
> *are wrapped in clouds again.*
> *I lift up streaming eyes in vain*
> *and feel upon my upturned face*
> *the streaming rain.*
> *—Ruth Bell Graham**

I long to go up in a little cable car and rise above it all, break out of the fog, see life from a higher perspective. I wish to experience that indescribable feeling of peace, security, power, stability, serenity—all that those mountains represent. Then I begin to catch a glimpse of the obvious. I do have a way out of the fog—whenever I choose to pray.

Lord, when my soul is weary
and my heart is tired and sore,
and I have that failing feeling
that I can't take it any more;
then let me know the freshening
found in simple, childlike prayer,
when the kneeling soul knows surely
that a listening Lord is there.
                    —Ruth Bell Graham*

PASS IT ON . . . As the fog descends on the valleys of life, may we allow His eternal presence to envelop and protect us.

*From *Sitting By My Laughing Fire* by Ruth Bell Graham, copyright © 1977 by Ruth Bell Graham; used by permission of Word Books, Publisher, Waco, Texas 76796.

Mother's Day

Can a mother forget the baby at her breast and have no compassion on the child she has borne? Though she may forget, I will not forget you!
— *Isaiah 49:15*

I AWOKE EARLY THAT SUNDAY MORNING to the sound of bells. The valley was alive with them—the tinkling of cowbells now in chorus with the tolling of church bells, calling the faithful to worship.

Opening the heavy wooden shutters and throwing open the window, I stood gazing in wonder at the beauty before me. It was one of those indescribable spring days that can only be experienced in the Alps. Bright sunshine reflecting off glorious snow-covered peaks; clean, crisp air; fields filled with wild flowers in every shade of purple, yellow, and blue. And the window boxes hanging from every window in the village (even from the barns) were a riot of color, almost gaudy in their extravagance—red and pink geraniums, yellow and orange marigolds, blue ageratum and petunias of every variety! A perfect setting for Mother's Day.

I thought of my small son asleep in his crib and, as I felt the delicate movements of the child within me, I was filled with warm emotion. Soon I would be a mother for the second time, and making this day even more special was the fact that my own mother had come to visit.

Slipping on my robe I gathered up my infant son who was just beginning to stir. In the kitchen Mother was already making *café au lait* and slicing the thick Swiss bread. As we sat sipping our coffee and talking, I experienced an overwhelming sense of gratitude and joy. For the first time we were sharing this day as mothers together.

With a smile Mother reached into her pocket and took out an envelope with a gift to me enclosed. I opened it and read:

> *It seems but yesterday*
> *you lay*
> *new in my arms.*
> *Into our lives you brought*

*sunshine
and laughter—
play—
showers, too,
and song.
Headstrong,
heartstrong,
gay,
tender beyond believing,
simple in faith,
clear-eyed,
shy,
eager for life—
you left us
rich in memories,
little wife.
And now today
I hear you say
words wise beyond your years.
I watch you play
with your small son,
tenderest of mothers.
Years slip away—
today
we are mothers
together.*
         —Ruth Bell Graham*

That was many Mother's Days ago, and the child that stirred within me that day is now a young woman, with bright hopes of her own. I reflect on how quickly the years have passed, and I realize with an ever grateful heart the privilege of gleaning from the experience and wisdom of my two grandmothers, of being "best friends" with my mother, and of gaining a mother-in-law who not only accepts me, but loves and encourages me.

PASS IT ON . . . Remember, dear child, God is a Father with a mother's heart.

---

*From *Sitting By My Laughing Fire* by Ruth Bell Graham, copyright © 1977 by Ruth Bell Graham; used by permission of Word Books, Publisher, Waco, Texas 76796.

The Tree

That they might be called the trees of righteousness, the planting of the Lord, that he might be glorified. — Isaiah 61:3

I CLUTCHED MY SHAWL tightly around me. The night air in Jerusalem can be quite chilly, especially in December. Standing on the balcony, I watched the stars twinkling brightly against the ebony sky and couldn't help wondering if the sky looked something like this on the night Jesus was born. I glanced in the direction of Bethlehem, which lay only a few miles away. Somehow it didn't seem much like Christmas.

There were no bright lights dangling from the street corners, no Christmas music blaring from the radio, no Santas in red suits, no Salvation Army lassies ringing bells, and, except for the busloads of tourists stopping to view the original Nativity scene, there was scant evidence of the celebration of the birth of Christ.

I surveyed the hills around me. In each window the Hanukkah candles gave off a soft glow, and the happy sounds of Israeli families celebrating the Festival of Lights drifted across the valley, a painful reminder of my own family thousands of miles away. Soon they would be gathering around the open fireplace, singing carols, and exchanging the gaily wrapped gifts under the Christmas tree.

I thought of the apartment where Stephan and I now lived, bare and devoid of all signs that Christmas was only a few days away. Here, it was impossible to purchase a tree, nor could we go into the hills and cut one that had been so lovingly planted by Jews from around the world in the successful land reclamation program. I sighed and turned to go in. Glancing again at the heavens, I breathed a quick prayer, asking the Lord to make this holy season unique and meaningful, helping me to focus on its true meaning.

The next day, as we left the apartment for a shopping trip, our neighbors hurried out to meet us.

"Would you like a Christmas tree?" they asked excitedly. "We have heard that on December 22nd, trees will be given away in the center of town. Knowing that you are Christians, we thought you might like one."

We thanked them and, on the designated day, went to select our tree. Attached to the trunk of the tall evergreen we chose was a tag which read: "With compliments of the Jewish Tourist Agency."

Collecting the ornaments was like a scavenger hunt. We found a string of lights in a dusty corner of a variety store; a few bright balls in another. We popped popcorn and lit candles. Soon our little home began to take on a festive air.

As I hung the ornaments and strung the popcorn, I couldn't help thinking of the heritage this little country had given me. My roots were not so much in my native North Carolina as here in this soil. *If only those who dwell in this land, His Land, could know that the Son of David is the Messiah who has chosen them from among all nations to be His people,* I thought.

I stood back and looked with satisfaction at the glowing tree. Here, in the land of Jesus' birth, among His people, experiencing my true roots, I realized that this special tree reminded me not only of Bethlehem, but of Calvary. From a cradle to a cross—for me and for all his "chosen" people.

My prayer was answered. Joy to the world, the Lord is come!

PASS IT ON . . . Each time you see a "special tree," think of His land and His people, and pray for the peace of Jerusalem. (See Ps. 122:6.)

The Green Ribbon

The righteous shall flourish like the palm tree: he shall grow like a cedar in Lebanon. Those that be planted in the house of the Lord shall flourish in the courts of our God. They shall still bring forth fruit in old age; they shall be fat and flourishing. — Psalm 92:12-14

*I*T WAS SATURDAY, Israel's day of worship. After church Stephan, the children, and I decided to drive out of the city and into the hills around Jerusalem. They are rugged and barren— beautiful in an almost mystical sort of way—and we never tired of exploring them.

After stopping at a small cafe for *pita* and *flaffle*, we found ourselves on the old dirt road that winds through the wilderness from Jerusalem down to the plains of Jericho. We pulled the car over to look at the hills of Moab silhouetted against the Eastern sky, and to watch the afternoon shadows playing eerie games of hide-and-seek with the deep ravines and steep precipices.

As I stood gazing at these ancient hills and soaking up their mysterious beauty, my eyes fell on a ribbon of lush greenery. It was so out of character, so cool and inviting in the midst of the heat and dust of the desert. All of a sudden I realized that here, in the middle of the wilderness, there must be an underground stream, providing nourishment and refreshment to the trees whose roots were firmly embedded along its banks.

Immediately Psalm 1 came to mind: "And he shall be like a tree planted by the rivers of water, that bringeth forth his fruit in his season; his leaf also shall not wither, and whatsoever he doeth shall prosper" (1:3).

How encouraging that even in times of dryness, even when I go through a desert experience, I can flourish and bear fruit if I am deeply rooted in the Source of living water.

PASS IT ON . . . Root yourself deep in Him so that you may never forget that you are only the channel and He is the Source.

Are You Free?

Stand fast therefore in the liberty with which Christ hath made us free.
— Galatians 5:1

"THERE ARE TWO PEOPLE in this world who make me nervous," said Basyle at dinner one evening, "and their names are Mama and Dada."

Then he went on to announce his plans for leaving home. Not having any idea what had inspired this outburst from our young son, we were a little surprised. But Berdjette, his six-year-old sister, was shocked!

"Basyle," she said indignantly, "that is what you call divorce! You are divorcing your mother and father!"

This information did not deter Basyle at all, and he proceeded to ask the baby sitter to help him pack. He believed that, if he moved in with the neighbors, he would be allowed to do as he pleased. To this four-year-old, leaving his parents and changing his environment meant freedom. Needless to say, he didn't get far!

I chuckled to myself as I tucked him into his own little bed that night, and I couldn't help thinking that a lot of adults are guilty of the same false hope. They, too, believe that running away from or changing their circumstances will produce freedom. What they fail to understand, apparently, is that they cannot run away from themselves.

It is virtually impossible to experience freedom if one is encumbered by sin and guilt, or burdened by failure and dissatisfaction. We have to experience release from all that has been. Though we cannot undo what has been done or erase all the scars or turn back the years, we can encounter and receive God's forgiveness and healing through Jesus Christ, knowing that "if the Son sets [us] free, [we] will be free indeed" (John 8:36).

But we also need freedom from and in our present circumstances. We need to be liberated from our endless searching, from our griping and discontent, from constant worry and anxiety, from boredom and the barrenness of busyness. This is a liberation that is experienced only when we are no longer controlled by ourselves or our desires and compulsions, but by the Holy Spirit.

If we have accepted God's forgiveness and have been released from the burdens of the past, and if the Holy Spirit is controlling our present, then we will be free to face the future unafraid, knowing that God is already there. We will be free to do and be all that God intended. If we are liberated from ourselves, then we will be free to minister to others, to glorify God, and to enjoy Him forever.

PASS IT ON . . . It is through a totally dedicated heart that we experience true liberation.

Falling Leaves

Consider the lilies of the field, how they grow; they toil not, neither do they spin. — Matthew 6:28

OUTSIDE, IT WAS COLD AND BLEAK. The wind howled around the corner of the house, blowing snow into high drifts. The ice clung bravely to the window, and I was glad to be warm and safe inside, protected from the winter storm.

I sat curled up in a chair, drinking hot tea, my overgrown sweater pulled snugly around me. Taking advantage of a few quiet moments, I watched as the fierce gusts of wind tossed the branches of the crab apple unmercifully against my windowpane.

As I gazed out the window, I noticed a strange thing—a bunch of dried leaves clinging stubbornly to the bare branches of an old oak tree. I sipped my tea and watched with interest and curiosity as those brown leaves tried so desperately to hold on.

How much they reminded me of myself, I thought with shame. I, too, have some ugly, dried-up "leaves" that continue to cling to me—an irritating habit, a negative attitude, a surge of selfishness, doubt, fear, impatience, ungratefulness. How diligently I work to pluck them off. And how discouraged I become when they stubbornly remain there.

I looked again at the tree. It wasn't struggling and striving to remove the dead leaves. It seemed to be resting in full and complete confidence that when spring came, the new sap would again flow through its branches, and those ugly, dead leaves would fall off by themselves.

So it is with my life. I simply need to dwell in the presence of Jesus Christ, abide in His Word, and be available to the life-giving power of the Holy Spirit, confident that as He begins to flow through me, all those ugly old habits that cling so persistently will begin to drop away by themselves, with no self-conscious effort on my part. And I will be able to walk in newness of life, and serve in newness of spirit. (See Rom. 6:4 and 7:6.)

PASS IT ON . . . May we allow the freshness of the Holy Spirit to flow through us, remembering the lilies . . . They simply *are.*

The tree seemed to be resting in full and complete confidence that when spring came, the new sap would again flow through its branches, and the ugly, dead leaves would fall.

The Problem

Let this mind be in you, which was also in Christ Jesus. — *Philippians 2:5*

I STOOD IN THE UPSTAIRS HALLWAY, looking down over the bannister and waiting for the younger children to come in for their baths. My oldest daughter, taking a piano lesson, was in the living room directly below, and the repetitive melody she was playing echoed through my mind. Standing there, I savored both the few moments of solitude and the aroma from the roast beef and apple pie already in the oven.

Suddenly the little ones bounded through the door. I cringed as I saw their muddy footprints on the white carpet and their filthy little hands leaving distinct imprints on the cream-colored walls. They bounced up to their rooms, cheeks flushed and eyes bright from their play.

I noticed, however, that one of my young sons was trudging slowly up the stairs, his head bowed, grubby hands covering his small, dirt-streaked face. When he reached the top, I asked him what was wrong.

"Aw, nothing," he replied.

"Then why are you holding your face in your hands?" I persisted.

"Oh, I was just praying."

Quite curious now, I asked what he was praying about.

"I can't tell you," he insisted, "because if I do, you'll be mad."

After much persuasion I convinced him that he could confide in me and that , whatever he told me, I would not get mad. So he explained that he was praying about a problem he had with his mind.

"A problem with your mind?" I asked, now more curious than ever, wondering what kind of problem a child of six could have with his mind. "What kind of problem?"

"Well," he said, "you see, every time I pass by the living room, I see my piano teacher, and my tongue sticks out."

Needless to say, it was hard to keep a straight face, but I took his problem seriously and assured him that God could, indeed, help him with it.

Later, on my knees beside the bathtub as I bathed this little fellow, I thought how I still struggle with the problem of controlling my mind and my tongue. All too often my mind focuses on the negative until negativism dominates my thoughts and actions, and I find myself being critical and unpleasant. Repeatedly I realize that I have said what I didn't mean to say, and haven't said what I really wanted to say— such as, "Thank you" or "Well done!" or even "I love you." All too often I focus on faults, while ignoring or forgetting the much-needed word of praise, encouragement, or appreciation.

That afternoon as I knelt to scrub that sturdy little body, the tub became my altar; the bathroom, my temple. I bowed my head, covered my face, and acknowledged that I, like my son, had a problem with my mind and tongue. I asked the Lord to forgive me and to give me more and more the mind and heart of Christ.

PASS IT ON . . . *May the mind of Christ my Savior*
Live in me from day to day,
By His love and power controlling
All I do and say.
                    —Kate B. Wilkinson

The Kiss

Precious in the sight of the Lord is the death of his saints. — Psalm 116:15

As SOON AS WE HEARD THE NEWS that LaoNaing had suffered a stroke, we left for North Carolina by plane. Upon arriving in Asheville, we went directly to the hospital, where we found my grandmother lying frail and helpless, attached to life-sustaining tubes and machines. We could sense her frustration and agitation and, although she could not speak, she made it known in no uncertain terms that she wished to go home.

After consulting the doctor, we made the decision to comply with her wishes, firmly convinced that her happiness was our first priority. As soon as she saw the familiar surroundings and was tucked safely into her own bed, she relaxed, and a peaceful expression replaced the one of strain and concern. We kept her as comfortable as possible and, knowing that she enjoyed our presence, someone always kept her company as well.

Since LaoNaing had loved music all her life, mother had a special tape made for her—hymns that would especially bless and encourage. Since my grandmother was aware that she was dying, the hymn she wished to hear over and over again was "The King Is Coming."

Each day she grew weaker. It was hard to see her fading slowly away, but she was ready and eager to meet her Lord and to rejoin loved ones who had gone before.

On the morning of November 7, 1974, she died—quietly and peacefully.

When I went to tell the children, little Tullian said, "Mama, LaoNaing had a hurt, and Jesus came and kissed it away." This two-year-old understood better than I the "homegoing" of a child of God. Thinking I was offering comfort, I found myself comforted.

I do not know when the Lord will come for me. I may live to a ripe old age like my grandmother, or He may choose to complete my life early. But I do know that He has provided for my eternal security through Jesus Christ and that until that day,

He provides for my daily life through the power of the Holy
Spirit.

> *As the portrait is unconscious*
> *of the master artist's touch,*
> *unaware of growing beauty,*
> *unaware of changing much,*
> *so you have not guessed His working*
> *in your life throughout each year,*
> *have not seen the growing beauty*
> *have not sensed it, Mother dear.*
> *We have seen and marveled greatly*
> *at the Master Artist's skill,*
> *marveled at the lovely picture*
> *daily growing lovelier still;*
> *watched His brush strokes*
> *change each feature*
> *to a likeness of His face,*
> *till in you we see the Master,*
> *feel His presence, glimpse His grace;*
> *pray the fragrance of His presence*
> *may through you seem doubly sweet,*
> *till your years on earth are ended*
> *and the portrait is complete.*
> *—Ruth Bell Graham**

PASS IT ON . . . "Sorrow not, even as others which have no
hope. For if we believe that Jesus died and rose again, even so
them which sleep in Jesus will God bring with him" (1 Thess.
4:13-14).

---

*From *Sitting By My Laughing Fire* by Ruth Bell Graham, copyright © 1977 by
Ruth Bell Graham; used by permission of Word Books, Publisher, Waco, Texas
76796.

The Rock

But grow in grace, and in the knowledge of our Lord and Savior Jesus Christ. — 2 Peter 3:18

I SAT UPSTAIRS BY MY bedroom window, reading and enjoying the spectacular view—brilliant red and gold fall foliage against a crisp blue sky. From somewhere, the faint scent of burning leaves drifted in through the open window, reminding me that it would soon be time to rake our yard.

The children, back from school, had quickly changed their clothes and rushed back outside to spend the rest of the afternoon playing football just beneath my window. Now I was watching them with pride and joy, thanking the Lord for their healthy minds and bodies. Suddenly I noticed that my eldest son was limping. I thought that perhaps he had developed a blister, and made a mental note to inquire later.

The shadows lengthened, and the air turned cooler as the late afternoon sun slowly began its descent. I grabbed a sweater and went downstairs to begin dinner preparations.

When the children came in to wash up for supper, I noticed that my son was still limping rather badly.

"What's wrong with your foot?" I asked.

"Oh, nothing," he shrugged. "I just have a rock in my shoe."

"Well," I said, "you've been limping all afternoon. Why don't you take the rock out?"

"Because, I put it there to remind myself to be nice to Basyle."

I quickly turned my head to hide the amusement in my eyes. But I had to admit that he had a point!

We may not need to put a rock in our shoe, but we can ask the Holy Spirit to make us more sensitive to His gentle reminders, taking more time to be quiet before Him, listening to Him. Perhaps the voice of the Lord will come through a friend or one of the children; maybe He can be heard through a message or book. But more often it is through His Word and in prayer that His still, small voice speaks to us when we fall short, and then brings encouragement, promising to give us the wisdom and strength to grow more and more like the person of Jesus Christ.

"And the spirit of the Lord shall rest upon him (her), the spirit of wisdom and understanding, the spirit of counsel and might, the spirit of knowledge and of the fear of the Lord" (Isa. 11:2).

PASS IT ON . . . May we seek to cultivate sensitivity to the work of the Holy Spirit in our lives.

We can ask the Holy Spirit to make us more sensitive to His gentle reminders.

How Do You Find The Time?

Reverence for God adds hours to each day. — *Proverbs 10:27 LB*

THE TELEPHONE RANG. The desperate voice on the other end belonged to a friend who asked imploringly, "How do you find time alone with the Lord with home and children demanding full attention all day, and much of the night as well?"

I laughed, and shared with her some of my own frustrations. There is no easy answer, no ideal solution, and each person must adapt to his or her individual circumstances.

I thought of the young mother whose only private time with the Lord was in the bathtub. Even then it had to be late at night, or the children would be clamoring at the door. Or the mother of three toddlers who was so frustrated trying to read her Bible that *she* finally crawled into the playpen!

I remembered my own mother, who, with five of us and daddy seldom home to help out, had precious little time for long devotions. Her solution was to keep her Bible open in a convenient place—a little desk, a corner table, the kitchen counter, or even the ironing board—so that, as she passed by, she could glean a promise or memorize a verse, then meditate upon it as she continued her work.

I thought of Paul who said, "Pray without ceasing" (1 Thess. 5:17). Mothers and other busy people have to be able to pray this way, or they would seldom pray!

There are times that I still become discouraged because I am unable to spend hours on my knees or engage in intensive Bible study. I have often found myself at the end of the day too exhausted to think, much less to pray or study my Bible. But, once again, I have found encouragement and comfort in the Scriptures. Moses, David, Elijah, Nehemiah, the thief on the cross, and many others offered brief, spontaneous prayers. Moans, sighs, thoughts, and even groans are spoken of and accepted as prayers by the Holy Spirit, Who takes these informal, incomplete utterings and interprets them before the throne of God. (See Rom. 8:26-27.)

The essence of what I shared with my friend that day was

this: I DON'T FIND THE TIME—I HAVE TO TAKE THE TIME! The Scripture says, "Here a little . . . there a little" (Isa. 28:10). So, while I am walking or driving, working around the house, going to sleep at night, or just before I get up in the morning, I take time to talk with the Lord or meditate on a portion of His Word. (See Deut. 6:7-9 and 11:18-20.) In order to face my daily tasks in His strength, I try to meet Him alone, even if only for a few moments, as often and as regularly as possible. The secret for me has been using small amounts of time that I call "Jesus Breaks."

My prayer is that I will always take advantage of even the smallest amount of time to be with Him, remembering what Brother Lawrence said as he went about his work in the monastery kitchen: "The time of business does not differ with me from the time of prayer; and in the noise and clutter of my kitchen I possess God in as great tranquillity as if I were on my knees."

PASS IT ON . . . Cultivate the habit of minute vacations, taken in the presence of Jesus.

Photograph by Don Young.

So much of what I know about the Lord and the Scriptures was learned right here in the living room of my childhood home in Montreat, North Carolina.

Mother introduced me to Jesus Christ, and at the age of four I gave my heart to Him. . . . This view of Little Piney Ridge, in the Blue Ridge Mountains, was one of my favorites. I could not know then that . . .

many years later, on a misty spring day, I would be thousands of miles away in the majestic Swiss Alps . . .

meeting the man who was to become my husband, Stephan Tchividjian, at the altar . . .

of an historic old church in Montreux, Switzerland.

God has blessed us with a large family. The older children, Berdjette and Stephen-Nelson, were born while we were living in Europe.

Little Graham Berdj Antony is number seven! We are currently at home in Florida.

Eldest daughter, Berdjette, is a constant delight, one of my best friends, and an inspiration to her younger brothers and sister.

At his graduation, Stephan-Nelson is pictured with "Daddy Bill." Following in his grandfather's footsteps?

The Billy Graham household was a joyful place in which to grow up. Shown here with my sisters—my friends—Bunny and Anne.

"*I will lift up mine eyes unto the hills, from whence cometh my help. My help cometh from the Lord, which made heaven and earth. . . . The Lord shall preserve thy going out and thy coming in from this time forth, and even for evermore.*"

(*Psa. 121:1-2, 8*)

Occasionally we return to the place of Stephan's birth and our first home in the picturesque country of Switzerland.

For my parents, life in the service of our Lord has meant thousands of good-byes—

"like many small deaths"—until the next joyous reunion.

My spiritual heritage is rich, indeed. For twenty-five years my maternal grandparents, the Nelson Bells, were missionaries to China . . .

And Grandmother Graham, before her death, took each of us—child, grandchild, great-grandchild—in her arms and gave us her personal blessing, saying, "Pass it on! Pass it on!"

Our family circle continues to widen and expand. Here, I am surrounded by my family. To my left and proceeding clockwise are little Jerushah, Tullian, Berdjette, Stephan-Nelson, Basyle, my husband Stephan, and Aram. Baby Antony is not pictured here.

"And so, I leave you for now with the challenge to pass it on and 'tell to the generation to come the praises of the Lord, and His strength . . . that the generation to come might know . . . that they should put their confidence in God, and . . . keep his commandments.'"

(Psa. 78:4, 6–7 NASB)

From the days of my childhood, when life revolved around my mother and daddy, I have come to learn the ways of the Lord with His children—His abundant love and mercy and grace.

For Fear Of. . .

You can throw the whole weight of your anxieties upon him, for you are his personal concern. — *1 Peter 5:7 Phillips*

I LAY IN BED IN THE last weeks of my pregnancy—my swollen abdomen a constant reminder that it wouldn't be long before the small cradle in the corner would be filled.

It was cold. The wind blew harshly, flinging snow and ice against the windowpane. I snuggled further under the cozy feather comforter, trying to keep warm.

I was conscious of the movements of my child, who seemed determined to exercise just when I wished to sleep. And oh, how I longed for sleep to obliterate the thoughts that kept forcing their way into my mind! I tried in vain to push them away but they persisted, causing a new and unfamiliar emotion—fear! Fear of childbirth!

I had given birth to five others with no misgivings or apprehension. Now, with only a few weeks to go until delivery, I was afraid. Why this time?

Perhaps I was just tired. After all, it was the end of a hectic day, and things always seem worse at night. I had read once that the "best bridge between despair and hope is a good night's sleep" and had even found this to be true many times. But try as I would, tonight I could not sleep.

I knew the Scriptures' teaching that fear does not come from God. (See 2 Tim. 1:7.) So I prayed: *Lord, please take this fear from me and fill me with Your calm assurance. Give me Your spirit of love and peace.*

Remembering how He had given me comfort and strength when I was carrying my other children, I thought of Isaiah 40:11: "He shall gently lead those that are with young." He had kept His promise with each one. But the fear continued to cling to me like the icicles clung to my window.

I don't know just how long I lay there—thinking, meditating, talking with the Lord. After some time had passed, I switched on the light and, taking my Bible from the bedside table, I opened it. Turning again to Isaiah and skimming the passages, my eyes fell on a verse I had never seen before. "I have made, and I will bear; even I will carry and will deliver you" (46:4).

I couldn't believe it! This was a verse for my condition, a verse that met my immediate need! How precious of the Lord. How true that as a father has compassion on his children, the Lord has compassion on us. (See Ps. 103:13).

I turned off the light, thanking God for showing me so clearly and definitely His tender love in the smallest detail of my life. Then "he gave to his beloved sleep" (Ps. 127:2).

A few weeks later I lay in the hospital, the pains of birth very real. But I remembered His promise. As always, He was faithful to keep it.

> He "carried,"
> He "bore," and, a few hours later,
> He "delivered" me of a beautiful baby girl.

PASS IT ON . . . The Lord always meets us at the point of our need and is "able to do exceeding abundantly above all that we ask or think" (Eph. 3:20).

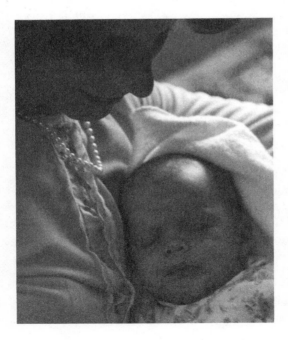

The author, with youngest daughter, Jerushah

Pass It On

When a good man [or woman dies], he [she] leaves an inheritance to his [her] grandchildren. — *Proverbs 13:22 LB*

SHE LOOKED SO SMALL and frail sitting on the edge of her bed. Snowy white hair framed her sweet face which, although lacking its usual color, was nonetheless radiant with peace and joy. Her tired, sunken eyes were still full of love and concern for each one who entered her room. In the last weeks of her life, she spoke often of the wonderful Christian heritage that had been hers and of her great privilege in passing that heritage on to her children and grandchildren. Her joy was complete, for all of her family loved the Lord Jesus.

As we approached her bedside, she somehow found strength that was not hers. Taking each one in her arms, she gave us a special verse or a personal blessing. Then, with deep conviction in her weak voice, she said, "Pass it on. Pass it on."

A few days later, Grandmother Graham died.

God in His sovereignty chose to place me in a Christian home, through which I received a godly heritage from both sides of the family. The privileges and responsibilities of passing on such a heritage are enormous. The Bible says, "To whom much is given, much is required."

Like a pebble thrown into a quiet lake, the ripples caused by the initial seed of godliness planted in a family and cultivated by the Holy Spirit become larger and broader, encompassing an ever-widening expanse. The cycle will continue, as long as we who have received such a heritage are faithful in our own personal walk with Jesus Christ and to our God-given responsibilities in our homes.

Think for a moment of how many people could be influenced by just one child reared to love and serve the Lord Jesus—a child who has been grounded in the living Word and has been given the examples of godly parents. The potential of faithful, God-fearing parents is unending, and the very thought should cause us to reverence our job and be grateful to God for the great privilege He has entrusted to us.

If you have not been blessed by a godly heritage, what an

opportunity could be yours—of beginning such a heritage for your children and grandchildren by making sure of your own relationship to Jesus Christ—and faithfully passing it on.

PASS IT ON . . . "The Lord himself is my inheritance . . . He guards all that is mine . . . What a wonderful inheritance! I will bless the Lord" (Ps. 16:5-7 LB).

Holy Audacity

Let us therefore come boldly unto the throne of grace, that we may obtain mercy, and find grace to help in time of need. — Hebrews 4:16

*F*AMILY, FRIENDS, AND DIGNITARIES—including the President of the United States—had gathered to show their love and respect for daddy, who was being honored in Charlotte, North Carolina.

Members of the immediate family were seated close to the front, behind a roped-off area. Security was tight. Standing at strict attention were uniformed policemen and secret service men in plain clothes. An air of excitement hung over the auditorium in anticipation of the President's arrival. Suddenly there was a flurry of activity as he entered, surrounded by his associates and bodyguards.

So intent were we on watching the proceedings that none of us noticed when four-year-old Basyle dashed under the ropes and past the policemen, the secret service men, and the bodyguards. Running directly to the President, he tugged on his sleeve. Startled, the man looked down into the small eager face.

"Are you the President?" asked Basyle.

Graciously the great man assured him that he was.

Amused and a bit embarrassed, we retrieved our young son. Several times during the program, daddy and the President glanced toward Basyle and chuckled.

Later, however, as I reflected on the incident, I couldn't help admiring the audacity of a four-year-old boy and comparing it with my own often timid approach to the King of Kings and Lord of Lords.

We are directed to "come boldly unto the throne of grace," yet, for various reasons, I hesitate. There is only "one mediator between God and men, the man Christ Jesus" (1 Tim. 2:5)—no ropes, no police, no secret service. Yet I allow the smallest obstacle—busyness, haste, worldly distraction—to hinder my entrance into the Holy of Holies.

Prayer has no boundaries except my failure to accept the open invitation to the throne of grace. I humbly acknowledge that, more often than I care to admit, my problem with prayer is prayer*less*ness, caused by my lack of authority over circumstances and my lack of audacity in approaching the King of Kings.

> *Come, my soul, thy suit prepare:*
> *Jesus loves to answer prayer;*
> *He himself has bid thee pray,*
> *Therefore will not say thee nay.*

> *Thou art coming to a King,*
> *Large petitions with thee bring;*
> *For his grace and power are such,*
> *None can ever ask too much.*
> *—John Newton*
> From *The Lutheran Hymnal*

PASS IT ON . . . The greatest problem with prayer is simply our failure to pray.

Too Loved To Leave

Herein is love, not that we loved God, but that he loved us. — *1 John 4:10*

MY LIFE SEEMS TO BE CHARACTERIZED, not so much as a "pilgrim's progress," but as a "struggler's struggles." Have you ever felt that you have disappointed the Lord so often that you don't see how He could love you? Have you ever been so discouraged that you contemplated giving up? Have you ever thought, "It just isn't possible for me to live the Christian life"? Well, I have.

Fortunately, the Lord is good, ready to forgive, full of compassion, and gracious. (See Ps. 86:5, 15.) And He has His own unique ways of reminding us that we are His and that He does love us.

Not long ago I met one of those rare individuals whom you recognize as a Christian by the expression on his face. His bright, contagious smile was only a reflection of a warm, loving personality. As he walked into the room and introduced himself, his whole being radiated Christ. But it had not always been so, as he explained to me one day.

A few years before, this man had accepted Christ as his Savior. Once he made his decision, he became an enthusiastic believer. His wife, however, just couldn't follow him in his new-found faith. So, after a couple of years of struggle, she asked him for a divorce, explaining that, since he had become so involved in his Christian faith, their lives had drifted apart.

"O.K., honey," he said kindly. "You go ahead and file. But I want to warn you that no court in the country will grant you a divorce."

A bit taken aback, she asked him why.

"Because," he replied with a twinkle in his eye, "no judge will grant a divorce to a woman whose husband loves her as much as I love you!"

Needless to say she did not go through with the divorce. And not long after this experience, she, too, was drawn to the Lord.

So it is with the Lord's love for us. His commitment to us is total and irrevocable. He loves us far too much to stop now—

even when we don't follow Him, even when we drift from Him, even when we fail or disappoint Him, even when we become so discouraged that we just can't go on. At such times we may feel His arms around us, drawing us into the stillness of His chambers (Song of Sol. 1:4) and leading us to the banqueting house (2:4), where we can feast on His encouragement and acceptance, and hear Him say, "Yea, I have loved thee with an everlasting love; therefore with lovingkindness have I drawn thee" (Jer. 31:3).

> *O love that wilt not let me go,*
> *I rest my weary soul in thee;*
> *I give thee back the life I owe,*
> *That in thine ocean depths its flow*
> *May richer, fuller be.*
> *—George Matheson*

PASS IT ON . . . God loves and accepts us just as we are, but He also loves us too much to leave us there.

A Bunch Of Busyness

I beseech you therefore, brethren, by the mercies of God, that ye present your bodies a living sacrifice, holy, acceptable unto God, which is your reasonable *service.* — *Romans 12:1, author's emphasis*

WHEN I ANSWERED THE PHONE, I listened to the distraught voice on the other end. Her plea sounded convincing and, though I really didn't have the time or the strength to take on another thing, I had agreed to her request before I realized what I was doing.

Looking at my calendar, I couldn't believe my eyes. A couple of weeks ago, it had been blank and I had looked forward to a relatively quiet month. Now, as I glanced over the white squares, I noticed that there was something marked for every day. I was once again in the position of being overcommitted.

How had it happened? Why do we find it so difficult to say no? And why do we feel guilty if we are not busy?

I remember one occasion when I was rushing home from an all-day meeting to prepare dinner for my large family. One of the ladies in the car turned to me and asked, "And just what do *you* do to keep busy?" I thought she was teasing. With seven children, two dogs, and a busy husband, the answer was obvious. My immediate reaction was to laugh, but I realized she was serious, and I was grateful that we were approaching her house so I could tactfully avoid a reply. The list would have been inexhaustible.

Being too busy has become a compulsion for many and a way of life for most of us, until the truly important things of life— thinking, meditating, reading to a child, showing tenderness toward a mate, listening to a teenager, taking time to encourage a friend—have all but been lost. We even tend to view the overactive, overcommitted Christian as some kind of super-saint, and running around being busy has become synonymous with spirituality.

A friend of mine once commented that any activity not directly inspired by the Holy Spirit is just "a bunch of busyness." This is confirmed in Romans 12:1, where we read that God wants us to be available to Him for "reasonable service." The word *reasonable* means "not excessive or extreme; moderate; possessing sound judgment" (Webster). This kind of service is holy and acceptable to Him. In Philippians 4, we find that we "should let our moderation [sweet reasonableness] be known to all men" (vs. 5). And in Proverbs 31:16 (*Amplified*): "She considers a new field *before* she buys or accepts it— *expanding prudently* [and not courting neglect of her duties by assuming others]. With her savings [of time and strength], she plants *fruitful* vines in her vineyard" (author's italics).

How can we avoid being bound by busyness? How can we learn and practice "reasonable service"? How can we protect ourselves from becoming overcommitted?

Another friend who teaches a Bible study found that many of the women in her group were suffering from this common problem and decided to teach them how to say no. One week she stood in front of the class and said, "It's simple. You put your tongue in the roof of your mouth, and you say *no*."

A sensible, well-balanced life is a testimony to God's harmony.

PASS IT ON . . . If the Devil can't make you bad, he often makes you busy!

The Storm

The Lord hath his way in the storm. — *Nahum 1:3*

I LAY ON THE SOFT WHITE SAND while the children played
happily in the surf nearby. Suddenly a shadow fell across my
face and awakened me from my reverie. I glanced up at the sky
and watched as the sun played hide-and-seek with the billowy
clouds. I closed my eyes again, basking in the sun's soothing
warmth, listening to the rhythm of the surf, and enjoying the
calm moment. How beautiful everything was, how quiet.

But soon another shadow fell and I looked up just in time to
see the sun disappearing behind a big thunderhead. I turned
my gaze to the ocean which only moments before had been a
bright mirror reflecting the blue sky. Now the whitecaps
danced restlessly, and the gray waves angrily pounded the
shore. The strong wind began to blow fine grains of sand
around me, and, before I could collect the children and run for
shelter, the heavens opened and the rain poured down. I was
amazed how quickly the storm had gathered.

As we sat huddled in the shelter, my mind wandered back to
another storm:

Jesus had had a busy day. Helping, healing, and teaching,
He was surrounded constantly by people. Now it was evening.
As Jesus gazed out over the peaceful blue of Lake Galilee, He
said to His disciples, "Let us pass over unto the other side."
They set out in a small boat and soon Jesus fell asleep.

While He was resting, a powerful storm arose. The waves
beat against the sides of the ship, filling it with water. The
disciples were afraid and cried out to Him, saying, "Master,
don't you care if we perish?" Jesus got up and looked out over
the sea. He saw the waves and felt the wind and said, "Peace,
be still." And all was calm again. Then He turned to His
disciples, "Why do you have so little faith?" (Mark 4:35-41,
author's paraphrase).

Storms arise in our lives, too.

A telephone call brings sudden jolting news.

A letter brings disappointment.

A child has an accident.

A small pain develops into a serious illness.

Death . . . divorce . . . financial reverses. Or maybe the source of distress is just the everyday pressures and tensions that build and build until the thunderhead erupts into a storm.

I, too, have had my share of storms. Some have been brief afternoon showers. Others have been caused by tensions that have built up, threatening my serenity and peace. Still others have burst upon my life suddenly, hitting hard and leaving in their wake damage and debris. Like the disciples, I have been afraid and have cried out, "Lord, don't you care?" And later, when all is calm again, I hear Him say, "Gigi, why do you have so little faith?"

You see, when the storms come, like the disciples, we often fail to:

1. *Rest in His presence.* He was right there in the boat with the disciples that day. And He is here with us. He has promised never to leave us nor to forsake us. His presence is a reality.

2. *Trust in His promises.* Jesus had told His disciples that they were going to the other side of the lake (Mark 4:35), and He was true to His promise. He has given us hundreds of promises in His Word, and we can trust Him to honor them.

3. *Rely upon His power.* The disciples had seen the power of Jesus demonstrated again and again, yet they failed to claim it. We have only to look about us and within us to know His power.

He has never promised a life free from storms, but He has promised to be with us in the midst of them and to bring us safely to the other side if we believe in Him and rely on Him.

PASS IT ON . . . It is possible to experience peace in the midst of the storm when we rely on Him. "He maketh the storm a calm" (Ps. 107:29).

The Devil's Calling Card

For thus saith the Lord God . . . In returning and rest shall ye be saved; in quietness and confidence shall be your strength. — Isaiah 30:15

*I*T WAS A LOVELY SUMMER EVENING, warm and inviting, as we gathered for dinner out on the terrace. There was the usual noise and commotion around the table, with six hungry children all clamoring to be served first and eager to relate their day's activities to their father who had just walked through the door.

As I reached for three-year-old Jerushah's plate, I realized that she was whispering something under her breath. Leaning down, I heard her saying, "Peace and quiet. Peace and quiet." I asked who had peace and quiet. Lifting her big green eyes to me reproachfully, she replied, "*Nobody* has peace and quiet."

I felt rebuked. Once again I had overextended myself both physically and emotionally until I knew I was not exhibiting a peaceful, quiet spirit.

A few days later, I boarded a plane on my way to fulfill yet another commitment. All of a sudden, I felt myself shaking all over. The trembling was so violent that, for a moment, I thought I would break apart. I looked down, but there was no visible evidence of what I was experiencing. My hands were steady, and no one was staring at me. To those around me, I probably seemed the image of serenity. Yet I knew differently. I was exhausted and my inner reserves were depleted. I closed my eyes and cried out to the Lord. Then I heard Him say, "The journey is too great for thee," and I was reminded of another who long ago had found himself in a similar predicament.

Elijah had just experienced a tremendous victory. (See 1 Kings 18-19.) Now he was thoroughly drained in body and soul. The Devil, who delights in attacking us when we're down, took full advantage of this situation to leave his calling card of discouragement at Elijah's door. Elijah was so disheartened that he said, "It is enough" and even "requested for himself that he might die" (v. 4).

Flying at 33,000 feet above the earth, I felt much like this man of God—so discouraged that I dreaded going on. I recalled how the Lord, in His infinite tenderness and mercy, had provided a prescription for discouragement. He recognized Elijah's fatigue and tenderly said, "The journey is too great for thee." He didn't scold or condemn Elijah. He didn't make him feel guilty or unworthy. Instead, because the Lord doesn't confuse physical weariness with spiritual weakness, He let Elijah sleep. While he slept, the Lord sent an angel to prepare "a little meal," and after Elijah had been physically restored and refreshed, he was ready to receive some much-needed insight. The Lord showed him a great wind, an earthquake, a fire—but He was not in any of these. After all the noise and commotion had died down, and the smoke and confusion had cleared, Elijah heard "a still, small voice." It was God.

Sitting on that plane, the Lord showed me that He was not to be found in a whirlwind of anxious activity, or in an earthquake of agitation, or in the fire of overcommitment and busyness that so quickly consumes—but in "gentle stillness." I felt His love and peace envelop me, and His strength continued to uphold me all the way home.

But some changes needed to be made in my life. Spiritually, this meant resting in His love; feasting on the Bread of Life and receiving more nourishment from the daily manna that He so faithfully provides; drinking deeply of the living Water and drawing from the well that never runs dry—spending more time in His presence.

Practically, I cut back on my outside activities, saying no even at the risk of being misunderstood. I took time to lie in the sun, read, enjoy my children, sit quietly with Stephan in the evening. And you know, not only did I meet the Lord in the place of "gentle stillness," but I discovered that it was where He had wanted me to be all along.

> *Speak, Lord, in the stillness,*
> *While I wait on Thee;*
> *Hush my heart to listen*
> *In expectancy.*
> *—E. May Grimes*

PASS IT ON . . . Allow the Lord to slow down your hurried pace, ease the pounding of your heart and mind, and touch your frayed nerves in the stillness of His presence.

The Birthday

Except ye be converted, and become as little children, ye shall not enter into the kingdom of heaven. — Matthew 18:3

IN OUR FAMILY OF TEN (seven children and three adults—I include Sarah Olinger, my dearest friend and housekeeper), there is often an opportunity to celebrate a birthday.

On these special days, we do our best to make the honoree feel loved and cherished. Other members of the family take over household chores, prepare favorite foods, and fulfill every wish within our abilities and resources.

On one such day we had spent a considerable amount of time selecting gifts from the "wish list." These were now carefully wrapped and placed on the table which was covered with the white lace cloth reserved for special occasions. Vividly colored birthday napkins and candles made it appear quite festive. Our youngest had gathered pink and yellow blossoms from the garden and had artfully arranged them around the table, placing the largest blooms at the place of the guest of honor. The crowning achievement was a magnificent birthday cake baked by Berdjette, who had spent hours decorating it with violets, roses, and daisies made of spun-sugar icing. Now it stood ready and waiting beside the mound of cheerfully wrapped presents.

The little boys were busy blowing up the balloons, huffing and puffing until their small faces were red. Of course, they interrupted one of us each time they had to tie a knot. But everyone was doing his or her best to make the day a happy surprise.

Between balloons, eight-year-old Tullian asked, "Mother, how many birthdays do you have?"

Though I understood that this was his way of asking how old I was, I decided to take his question literally. "I have two birthdays, Tullian," I replied, "and so do you. Could you guess why?"

Puzzled, he shook his head, so I continued. "I carried you close to my heart for nine months before you were ready to be born. And the day I went to the hospital to give birth to you was your physical birthday—the one we celebrate with cake and presents. But you have another. The day you asked Jesus to come into your heart was the day you were 'born again.' That day is your spiritual birthday."

By this time all the children had gathered round, listening raptly. Little Jerushah piped up in her small voice, "Mama, is being born again when we are in God's tummy?"

I hugged her, marveling that these little children could accept a vital truth so simply and easily, while "grown-ups" often struggle with the concept of the New Birth.

The aroma emanating from the kitchen told us dinner was ready, so we quickly put the finishing touches on the party preparations and changed into our good clothes. A few minutes later we gathered around the table and sang our version of the familiar birthday song:

> *Happy birthday to you!*
> *Only one will not do.*
> *"Born again" means salvation—*
> *How many have you?*

PASS IT ON . . . As my faith deepens and matures, let it never lose the freshness of childlike trust and acceptance.

I'll Be Dogged If I Will

Cast thy burden upon the Lord, and he shall sustain thee. — *Psalm 55:22*

*A*UNT CECILE WAS A FEISTY LITTLE LADY who lived a few houses from us when I was growing up. She had soft white hair which framed her angelic face, and a laugh that was contagious. Everyone loved Aunt Cecile and enjoyed being around her. I especially found in her a kindred spirit. I appreciated her zestful approach to life, and her honest, down-to-earth way of expressing herself.

She had raised her family of six children in Korea where she and her husband served the Lord as missionaries. On top of her mission duties, and those of wife and mother, she also played the piano for the church services.

One Sunday morning, after getting her brood fed and dressed for church, she was exhausted. She sat down at the piano waiting for the hymn number to be announced. The pastor rose and said, "Mrs. Coit will now play 'Oh, Sweet Day of Rest and Gladness.'" Aunt Cecile got up slowly from the piano bench, looked the pastor straight in the eye, and said emphatically, "I'll be dogged if I will." With that, she sat down.

Not long ago, I had "one of those days." I had worked hard, been interrupted umpteen times, settled scores of arguments, and tried to be sweet and patient even though I felt anything *but*! After dinner I was cleaning the top of our glass dinner table (a dumb table to have with seven children) and, all of a sudden, everything got to me—the grease spots on the table, the kids fighting, the telephone ringing, the teenager talking, the TV— everything! So, I threw down the towel, and ran to my room in a flood of frustrated tears, declaring as I went, "I quit."

As much as I love and enjoy my calling of wife and mother, I would not be honest if I didn't admit that there are days when enough is enough, and I want to put my hands on my hips and declare, "I'll be dogged if I will!"

So I have learned to run to the Lord and pour out my honest feelings. I don't try to hide from Him my anger or self-pity or frustrations. He knows all about them, anyway. (See Ps. 44:21.)

I simply tell Him when I feel misunderstood or when I don't have strength for all the demands placed on me or when I feel insignificant or taken for granted. Like David, I confess that I am overwhelmed. (See Ps. 61:2.) And though it is often the trivial things that overwhelm us, the Lord knew there would be such days, and daily bears us up (Ps. 68:19 RSV) without ever condemning or comparing our seemingly insignificant trials with those unbelievable burdens other dear ones are called upon to bear.

Whatever size the trial, whatever the weakness, He is our inexhaustible source of strength and invites us, "Come to me, all of you who are weary" (Matt. 11:28 Phillips).

PASS IT ON . . . There is no need too large or too small that He is unable to meet.

I Bother Him

God is always at work in you to make you willing and able to obey his own purpose. — Philippians 2:13 TEV

AT FIVE O'CLOCK IN THE AFTERNOON things were hectic in the kitchen, where I was busy getting supper ready for nine hungry people, whose tummies never fail to know when it is dinner time.

As I turned toward the stove, I bumped into my four-year-old son, who was standing right in the way. His little blond head barely reached the top of the stove where I was frantically stirring the gravy.

"Aram," I said, "you had better move out of Mama's way before you get hurt."

I went on about my work and, a couple of minutes later, I bumped into him again. He hadn't budged an inch.

"Aram," I warned again, this time more firmly, "I asked you to move."

I went to the refrigerator and, turning back to the stove, banged into the little fellow again. This time I was irritated.

"Aram," I said firmly, "this house is big enough for the both of us, so why don't you go into the other room to play?"

But, as I turned once again, he was still there. I had had it!

"Aram," I scolded, "are you going to move out of Mama's way so I can get my work done?"

He looked at me with his innocent blue eyes and said, "Nope! I'm just going to stand here and bother you."

I couldn't keep from smiling as I ushered him out of the room. And later, when I had time to think about this incident, I wondered if this isn't exactly what I do with the Lord. I ask Him to work in my life, but all too often His work is hindered because I stand in His way and "bother" Him. The most irritating obstacle to my Christian growth, and the most difficult one to remove, is *me*.

PASS IT ON . . . May I never hinder the Lord's work in my life, remembering that it is for my good and His glory.

You Don't Have To Be Perfect

I don't mean to say I am perfect. I haven't learned all that I should even yet, but I keep working toward that day when I will finally be all that Christ saved me for and wants me to be. — *Philippians 3:12 LB*

"GIGI, YOU'RE NEVER GOING to make it," the Devil whispered in my ear.

Try as I would, I could never quite measure up to all I thought the Lord wanted me to be, or all *I* thought I should be. Satan, taking full advantage of my doubt, kept me in a constant state of despair. And I believed him, envying those lovely, godly women with the gentle spirits, whom the Lord loves. (See 1 Pet. 3:4.)

Some people just seem to have an easy time living the Christian life. Not me! And, after leaving his calling card of discouragement on the doorstep of my heart, Satan also convinced me that since I was not "perfect" I certainly had no right to minister to others. So I pulled a shell of low self-esteem about myself, cringing each time I was asked to share my faith. I felt like such a spiritual failure that it would have been hypocritical to share something I didn't believe I possessed. I remained in this state of spiritual insecurity for several years, always striving, yet continuing to fail.

One day two of my younger children, who had been playing in the yard, came running into the kitchen, their eyes bright with excitement, their little hands hidden behind their backs. Laughing with delight, they produced a large bunch of "flowers" they had gathered from the yard. I showed my surprise and joy with a big hug for each one, and ran to find a vase.

As I hurriedly arranged a bouquet, the flowers kept tumbling out. Then I noticed that the stems were all too short. The children had picked only the blossoms! I laughed to myself, thinking how much I had been blessed by their gift of love, however imperfect.

Suddenly a beautiful realization dawned—*We don't have to be perfect to be a blessing.* We are asked only to be real, trusting in

His perfection to cover our imperfection, knowing that one day we will finally be all that Christ saved us for and wants us to be.

PASS IT ON . . . You don't have to be a model of perfection, but you do have to be real.

My children have taught me that one doesn't have to be perfect to be a blessing.

Wearily, Wearily I Say Unto You

My presence shall go with thee, and I will give thee rest. — *Exodus 33:14*

On a day when I was feeling particularly tired, I decided to look up the word *weariness* in *Webster's Dictionary*. The definition read: "Worn out in strength, endurance, vigor or freshness. Having one's patience, tolerance, or pleasure exhausted."

It almost sounds as if Webster were describing a busy mother, doesn't it? And with a large family and all that goes with such a lifestyle, it is not unusual for me to find myself in this state. But weariness is not always limited to the physical. I often find that my emotions and my spirit suffer as well. Sometimes I am emotionally drained or spiritually discouraged—and I am not alone or unique.

The world is full of weary people. Many are work-weary—feeling unequal to the demands of their jobs. But there are just as many who are beaten down by worry, disappointment, and despair. Some find so little meaning in their lives that they wonder why they are existing and, devoid of hope, many wish they weren't. Others are simply bored to death—tired of having their hopes dashed again and again, chasing rainbows that afford only temporal pleasure and satisfaction. Still others are frustrated spiritually because of moral defeats, weary of struggling with the heavy burden of guilt, of trying to appease their consciences in one way or another. And there are those who are mentally exhausted, tired of trying to explain, defend, and explain again—sick of wearing masks, of trying to be something they are not.

Christians are not immune to weariness, either external or internal. But the difference is that we know to Whom to go (Jesus Christ) and where to go (His Word) for much-needed rest and refreshment.

Long ago Jesus said, "Come aside . . . and rest awhile . . . Come unto me, all ye that labor and are heavy laden, and I will give you rest" (Mark 6:31; Matt. 11:28). The rest that Christ gives is real and can be yours and mine, but we have to appropriate it. In Jesus Christ, there is certain rest, and to those who love Him and put their trust in Him, He promises, "As thy days, so shall thy strength be."

> *Art thou weary, art thou languid,*
> *Art thou sore distressed?*
> *"Come to me," saith One, "and in coming,*
> *Be at rest."*

PASS IT ON . . . St. Augustine said: "O God, thou hast made us for Thyself, and our hearts are restless until they rest in Thee."

The Burr

Do all things without grumbling. — *Philippians 2:14 NASB*

*T*HE STORY IS TOLD OF A MAN and an old hound dog. When the man pulled up in front of a country store, he noticed the dog howling on the front porch. Eying him curiously, the man went on inside. Several minutes later the dog was still howling.

When the customer was ready to pay for his purchases, he asked the old man at the cash register, "What's the matter with your dog?"

"Oh," shrugged the clerk, "he's probably just sitting on a cocklebur."

"Well," asked the visitor, "why doesn't he get off?"

The old man grinned and replied, "Guess he'd rather howl."

This old hound dog reminds me of some people I know, including myself. Some people seem to howl about everything. Just listen the next time you are standing in line at the grocery store or sitting at the beauty shop. I hear complaints about everything and everyone, from the President to movie stars. I hear a lot more complaining than I do expressions of gratitude. Howling seems to have become a way of life.

Satan loves to fill our lives with burrs, and he knows just how to place them where they will be the most irritating and the most uncomfortable—long lines at the checkout counter, a grumpy neighbor, a broken washing machine, a gas gauge that reads "Empty" when you are in a hurry. Some burrs take the form of tedious chores and responsibilities. Others are disguised as a negative attitude or a sharp tongue. And there are even two-legged burrs—people who make demands on our time and energy when it is already depleted. Some burrs prick all-too-sensitive feelings, and others attack spiritually.

When I am bothered by burrs, I find myself doing everything but what I should do. I talk about them. I complain about them. I worry about them. I lose sleep over them. I even find that I often howl more than I pray about them.

In the Old Testament we are taught that "howling" is a sin that reaps serious consequences. An entire generation of

Israelites wandered for forty years in the desert and were not allowed to enter the Promised Land because of their complaining. "Neither murmur ye as some of them also murmured and were destroyed" (1 Cor. 10:10).

The Scripture also tells us how to overcome the habit of howling. "Fix your thoughts on what is true and good and right. Think about things that are pure and lovely, and dwell on the fine, good things in others. Think about all you can praise God for and be glad about" (Phil. 4:8 LB).

Not long ago I had a burr in my life that caused me much irritation, and I howled loud and long. Finally I gave up. *Lord, I prayed, I'm tired of this burr, but I'm even more tired of howling about it.* So I began to thank Him and praise him for what He was doing in my life through this burr. To my amazement I found that, although the burr was still there, it had lost its power to irritate.

PASS IT ON . . . Give Him your burrs, and He will give you the grace to overcome the habit of howling.

A Time For Everything

Every purpose has its proper time. — Ecclesiastes. 3:17a NEB

LORD,
*Solomon said that there was
"A time for everything."
I wonder if he knew about
sticky fingerprints,
car pools,
letters to write, and
school programs to attend.
About cleaning a bathroom after
a four-year-old's bath.
About bubble gum in hair just before church,
or Christmas tree needles in the carpet.
About oil changes
and broken washing machines.
About waiting for the UPS man or
sitting in the doctor's office.
About sandpiles
and mud pies,
baseball practice
and talking to teens.
About answering the questions of a six-year-old.
About smelly gym clothes
or the neighbor's dog that likes our garbage.
About fast-growing weeds,
wet towels,
and ringing telephones.
Maybe Solomon didn't—
But You do!*
        —Gigi Graham Tchividjian

PASS IT ON . . . The Lord has provided ample time for all *His* plans and purposes. The secret to the successful use of this gift is to put Him first.

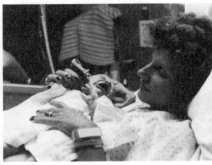

A time to . . .

Love
Play
Give birth
Bring baby home
Celebrate
Enjoy family life
Serve

(from top, clockwise)

The Day The Sandman Came

The fruit of the Spirit is . . . patience. — *Galatians 5:20*

THE AFTERNOON THUNDERSTORM had rolled on and the sun was out once again. Soon the children would crawl out from various corners of the house like so many little bugs after dark. Summer was only half over, and I had six more weeks to try to find creative ways to entertain six energetic children.

Suddenly I spotted the old sandbox.

"Let's fix it up!" I announced.

After gathering the troops, we pulled weeds and cleaned up the area. Then we were off to the local sand company. We had been told that our sandbox would require about five tons of sand. Not really knowing how much five tons would be, we took the van, loaded with buckets and old garbage cans.

With our containers filled, we returned home. Our son backed the van around, leaving a few tire tracks in the wet grass. He dumped the sand and drove back across the grass, this time breaking off a small tree limb in the process and receiving a sharp tongue-lashing from me.

When we looked at the sandbox, we saw that the sand filled only one small corner! A quick call to the company confirmed that, for a small fee, they would deliver the remaining sand that very afternoon, but I cautioned them to send their lightest truck and their best driver, as the yard was wet from the recent heavy rains.

When the truck arrived, I showed the driver where the sandbox was located and, as he began to back around the house, I followed. To my dismay, the truck loaded with sand was making deep trenches in the soft ground. Maneuvering the rear of the truck into position, he took several large branches from overhanging trees. Oh, well! Maybe the children's enjoyment of their sandbox would be worth all the trouble!

Then it happened. The driver got stuck in the wet earth. The more he accelerated, the deeper he sank, until his big truck began to slide down the hill toward the lake, plowing a gaping hole on its way. By now, he was up to his axles, and I suggested we call the sand company and ask for help.

An hour later, a large tow truck arrived. The driver backed around, leaving more black trenches, and put a cable around truck No. 1. The more he tugged and pulled, the larger grew the hole. Then he, too, got stuck, digging into the yard, breaking sprinkler pipes and branches, and uprooting small trees. Another call to the company resulted in truck No. 3, the cab of an eighteen-wheeler!

About eight o'clock, after five-and-a-half hours of destruction, all three trucks pulled out of our yard. When we assessed the damage, there was the gaping hole, the broken pipes sticking up like so many broken bones, ugly black tracks, ripped trees, five tons of sand—not *in*, but *beside* the sandbox— and a bill for the sand and two tow trucks!

Much later, as I was tucking in the eight-year-old, he prayed: "And thank You, Lord, for the exciting day and for all the entertainment we had!"

In spite of everything, I had to chuckle. No wonder the Scriptures entreat us to be more like children!

PASS IT ON . . . "Knowing this, that the trying of your faith worketh patience. But let patience have her perfect work" (Jas. 1:3-4). Barclay says this means the ability to take a tragedy and turn it into a glory.

Even This?

Serve the Lord with a heart of devotion . . . Do not be proud, but accept humble duties. — Romans 12:11, 16

*T*HOUGH EARLY MORNING is not my best time of day, after a couple of cups of coffee, I managed to fix breakfast, wash the dishes, and usher six children out the door to school before heading for the laundry room.

I stopped abruptly at the door and stood gazing in disbelief at the mountain of dirty clothes that represented a minimum of three loads of wash. Hadn't I just washed three loads yesterday? Sudden tears of frustration stung my eyes. I quickly brushed them away, a bit ashamed of myself, and put the first load in the washer.

Then I continued to tidy up, picking up the morning newspaper and various cups and glasses left from snacks the night before. Wiping a fingerprint here and there, I straightened beds and collected odd socks and shoes, school papers, and books. Soon I found myself in my son's bathroom, scrubbing the tub. Once again the tears insisted on imposing themselves against my will. This time they found little resistance. I was frustrated and discouraged, and my self-esteem was about as low as it could get.

It was still morning, but I was tired—weary of the mundane routine that made up my day and characterized much of my life. I was tired of the same mess day after day—of washing clothes that only yesterday I had folded and returned to their proper places; of wiping sticky fingerprints from the windows and mopping the same floors again and again; of doing the dishes, only to get them out a short time later to reset the table. I was sick of spending hours cooking a meal that was consumed in minutes.

Sitting in the middle of the bathroom floor, sponge and cleanser in hand and tears streaming down my cheeks, I found myself fussing, crying, and praying all at the same time.

God in His loving kindness came to meet me. (See Ps. 59:10 NASB.) Quietly and clearly I heard Him say, "Inasmuch as ye have done it unto one of the least of these . . . ye have done it unto me" (Matt. 25:40).

"Lord, even this?" I asked.

"Especially this," He replied. "Who else is going to do it for me? In all these small ways, you are serving Me."

Lovingly reassured and encouraged, I dried my tears and continued to scrub the tub.

PASS IT ON . . . Offered to the Lord, our routine days and mundane responsibilities become a celebration of praise and adoration.

They Forgot The Garbage

I give you this piece of advice to each one of you. Don't cherish exaggerated ideas of yourself or your importance, but try to have a sane estimate of your capabilities by the light of the faith that God has given to you all. — Romans 12:3 Phillips

*F*OLLOWING AN INVITATION to speak at one of the largest churches on the West Coast, I prayed about it, then accepted with much fear and trepidation.

When I arrived I was met at the airport and chauffeured to a lovely hotel, where I was given a suite of rooms. No expense had been spared to make me feel comfortable and cherished.

The next day I was ushered into the sanctuary of this prestigious church to address between four and five thousand women. The Lord gave me His strength and graciously saw me through.

Public speaking does not come naturally or easily for me, but it is a bit easier on my pride when I live on one side of the country and speak on the other. You see, often strangers who hear me speak think I'm wonderful. It is reassuring to know that I can get on a plane and leave before they find out that I am not.

Several days and as many engagements later, I returned home, arriving after midnight. I was exhausted from the strenuous schedule, and, while Stephan carried my suitcase to our room, I stepped into the kitchen to get something cool to drink.

Then I saw it. The garbage can was full and spilling over— and the next day was garbage pickup day. The children had forgotten to empty the trash again. I was annoyed to say the least. I sighed, picked up the can, and carried it outside.

Later, as I stood at the sink drinking my glass of juice, I couldn't help smiling to myself. The Lord has His own unique. and delightful ways of keeping me humble and quickly bringing me back to reality.

I thanked Him and went on to bed, ready to meet my ordinary, routine week with joy and anticipation.

PASS IT ON . . . We will avoid the danger of thinking too highly of ourselves if we remember that it is only by the grace of God that we are what we are.

My kitchen, where "divine services are conducted daily."

Failure Isn't Final

The Lord will perfect that which concerneth me. — *Psalm 138:8*

THIS TIME I HAD really blown it! It was one of those days you wish could be wiped off the calendar!

Since we had experienced flood damage, the carpet men had been at the house all day, replacing water-stained carpet. With everything removed from the rooms, I had decided to do some thorough cleaning and, as usual, I over-extended myself. By supper time I was totally exhausted. McDonald's would just have to do the cooking! So when everyone was ready, we piled into the car.

On the way Stephan had to stop at the bank and, while he ran in, I double-parked. Glancing in my rear view mirror, I saw a large, older-model car, driven by an elderly lady with flaming red hair and a face that matched. She was becoming increasingly agitated. I was just about to move the car up when she blasted her horn.

I don't know what possessed me, but after my whirlwind day, this was the last straw! I decided not to move. She gave another long, loud blast which just reinforced my stubborn refusal to budge, and I motioned for her to pass me. As angry as she was, she managed to maneuver the big car around and pulled up beside me. Then she lowered her window and began to yell. I blew her a kiss. That did it! She screamed, then stuck out her tongue.

By this time she was out of her car, threatening me and calling me names, attracting the attention of people passing by. Suddenly I wanted to crawl into a hole. The red-headed grandmother returned to her car, and Stephan appeared, wondering what the commotion was all about. We continued on to McDonald's, but I was too distraught to eat.

Amy Carmichael once said, "The best thing for our ease, loving souls, is to be made thoroughly ashamed of ourselves." I was ashamed, all right! So ashamed that, for several nights, I had a hard time sleeping. Although I hadn't lost my temper or been rude, I had been stubborn and selfish, insensitive and un-Christlike. I prayed for the little lady with the flaming hair, wishing I could apologize to her. I was sorry I had allowed my human nature to drown out the quiet, gentle voice of the Holy Spirit Who was prodding me to demonstrate the love of Christ. Jesus would have moved the car. I had failed Him again.

But as Jill Briscoe stated in her book *How to Fail Successfully:* "It is hard to remember when you're down physically and have blown it spiritually, when you're wiped out emotionally and feel ostracized socially—that FAILURE ISN'T FINAL!"

I was grateful for a Lord Who knows how frail we are, Who stands ready to forgive and forget our failures. He doesn't want us to become discouraged or paralyzed by them, but to confess them, accept His forgiveness, and learn from them.

PASS IT ON . . . True Christian character is tested, not so much by our *actions* as by our *reactions*.

Missing Pieces

Though he fall, he shall not be utterly cast down; for the Lord upholdeth him with his hand. — *Psalm 37:24.*

I LOOKED OUT OVER the deep blue of the Caribbean, its mirrored surface broken only by an occasional sailboat gliding past. Stephan was swimming in the pool, his strong, sure strokes taking him back and forth in the cool water. How grateful I was for this time of rest and intimacy.

As I lay under the tropical sun, I recalled a story my mother tells of a man she once met while vacationing in this very spot.

He was an interesting and slightly eccentric character—an archaeologist with a passion for broken china. Most of us don't have much patience with such things, and broken dishes usually get thrown out with the trash. To this man, however, they represented a challenge. In fact, he had built an entire house from all the old discarded scraps and bric-a-brac he could find. And although it was quite a monstrosity, to his mind he had created a thing of beauty. He then sifted through the dirt around his home, collecting bits and pieces of pottery and glass and patiently gluing them back together.

Once, while visiting, mother asked if she might have a sample of his work. Delighted, he went to select one of his more "perfect" specimens. She said that she would much prefer to have one that was cracked, marred, even one that was incomplete. He looked puzzled.

"You see," she explained, "You remind me of God, who so carefully and lovingly takes the broken fragments of our lives and puts them together again. Here and there a piece may be missing—a death, a divorce, an accident, wrong choices. But God takes the pieces of our shattered lives and makes us whole and complete again."

I love that story, because I believe it applies to all of us. No one is perfect. We are all marred in some way. We have all failed, made mistakes, known defeat and disappointment. Many of us have been physically or emotionally crushed.

But God looks beyond our faults and sees our needs. Tenderly, patiently He sifts through the debris, lifts His broken creature and brings healing and wholeness. And if a piece is still missing, His strength and love are sufficient.

PASS IT ON . . . His perfection meets the deep needs of our being. His completeness flows around our incompleteness and we are complete in Him (Col. 2:9-10).

The Argument

Therefore, as God's chosen people, holy and dearly loved, clothe yourselves with compassion, kindness, humility, gentleness and patience. Bear with each other and forgive whatever grievances you may have against one another. Forgive as the Lord forgave you. And over all these virtues put on love which binds them all together in perfect unity. — Colossians 3:12-14 NIV

HE WALKED OUT, closing the door firmly behind him. I heard the car drive away and, with a heavy, aching heart, I leaned against the closed door. Hot, angry tears filled my eyes, spilled over, and ran down my cheeks.

How had it happened? How had things built to this point? Neither of us had intended for our little discussion to develop into such a heated disagreement. But it was late, and we had both experienced a hard day.

Stephan had risen early to drive one of the car pools. Then he had seen several patients with difficult, heart-breaking problems. An emergency had taken up his lunch break, so he had been behind schedule for the rest of the afternoon. When he finally left the office, he hit a traffic jam on the freeway, arriving home tense and tired to a wife and seven children all demanding his attention.

I, too, had endured a difficult day after a sleepless night with the baby. Besides the normal activities involved with running a home, the rain had kept us confined indoors all day. It was hot and humid, and the children were more quarrelsome than usual, amusing themselves by picking on each other. Between settling arguments and soothing hurt feelings, I managed to get dinner on the table, but I hadn't taken the time to comb my hair or freshen my make-up, and Stephan could sense my frustration when he came in.

Finally, when the kitchen was clean, the small children bathed and tucked into bed, and the teenagers talked out, Stephan and I found ourselves alone in our bedroom, trying to discuss a minor problem. It soon blew out of proportion. Angry feelings were vented, words spoken that we did not mean, and then—the slammed door and retreating car.

I slumped into a chair, dissolving into tears of discouragement and disappointment in myself. How long was it going to take to learn my lesson? The late-night hours after a long day is not the best time for discussion, but for comfort, encouragement, and loving. As I sat there, I remembered that I had been so busy trying to handle the home front, keeping everything and everyone under control, that I had not spent time with the Lord that day. I realized that I had even failed to pray for Stephan. No wonder things had not gone well for him.

I glanced in the mirror and saw red, puffy eyes, no make-up, and hair in disarray. I saw lines of fatigue and tension where there should have been tenderness and love, and I understood Stephan's desire to get away and cool off.

I fell on my knees beside the chair, asking the Lord to forgive me and to fill me with His Holy Spirit so I could be to Stephan all he had ever dreamed. I asked for His strength, His sensitivity, His wisdom so I could juggle my own schedule, the demands of my home and children, and still have time to meet my husband's needs when he came home from the day's work. Then I added a timid P.S., asking Him to give Stephan a change of heart, too.

I felt peace and a sudden refreshing. I got up, washed my face, adding a little color to my cheeks and lips, combed my hair, lavishly sprayed perfume on myself, and climbed into bed to wait.

Presently I heard the front door open and familiar footsteps in the brick hallway. Our bedroom door opened quietly and Stephan stood there, his tired face and kind, loving eyes drawing me like a magnet. I flew into his arms. Later, our loving erased the last traces of frustration and anger. Clinging to each other as we fell into a much-needed sleep, I couldn't help wondering why we hadn't thought of this in the first place.

You look at me
and see
my flaws;
I look at you
and see
flaws, too.
Those who love,
know love

deserves
a second glance;
each failure serves
another chance.
Love looks to see,
beyond the scars
and flaws,
the cause;
and scars become
an honorable badge
of battles fought
and won—
(or lost)
but fought!
The product,
not the cost,
is what love sought.

* * *

God help us see
beyond the now
to the before,
and note with tenderness
what lies between
—and love the more!
   — Ruth Bell Graham*

PASS IT ON . . . "Marriage is the union of two good forgivers." —Robert Quillen

From *Sitting By My Laughing Fire* by Ruth Bell Graham, copyright © 1977 by Ruth Bell Graham; used by permission of Word Books, Publisher, Waco, Texas 76796

SOME PRACTICAL SUGGESTIONS
FOR PEACEMAKING

Avoid discussion at night, or when tired.

When you discuss important matters, always look your best.

Agree to differ, but resolve always to love.

Pray five minutes each day for the other, keeping in mind his or her unique problems and needs.

Occasionally reread 1 Corinthians 13, substituting your name for the word love.

The Vase

Behold, I make all things new. — Revelation 21:5.

WHILE DRESSING FOR DINNER, I could hear the screaming and arguing all the way to my bedroom. It sounded serious, so I ran to investigate. (I find being a "policewoman" the most distasteful part of motherhood.)

I arrived just in time to see one son throw a flower vase at another. The vase flew past his head and landed with a loud crash on the brick terrace. A hush fell as they looked up and found me standing in the doorway, staring at the fragments of broken pottery. After a scolding in which I expressed my disappointment at their behavior and my regret over the shattered vase, I returned to my room, leaving them a bit subdued.

Later as I passed the terrace, I saw the two culprits, their heads bent together over what had once been the vase. With a large pot of glue on the floor beside them, the two little fellows were patiently trying to piece it back together. They had made a mistake, but they were sorry and were doing their best to repair the damage.

I stood there for a moment thinking of all the times that I, too, have caused damage. How often, because of lack of self-control, have I hurled harsh words and broken a heart or fractured a relationship? How often has my insensitivity shattered someone's self-esteem or injured an ego? How often have I crushed a child's will or smashed his pride? How often have I damaged self-confidence and caused discouragement by harping on faults instead of praising a job well done?

Observing my children that day, I learned an invaluable lesson. Yes, we do make mistakes, but God is in the restoring business. And whatever the mistake—whether large or small, seemingly insignificant or fraught with serious consequences—we can humbly acknowledge our faults, repent, and do everything possible to repair the damage, trusting Him to "make all things new."

PASS IT ON . . . Never let the sense of the irreparable cause you to despair. Give your mistakes to the Lord and allow Him to "make all things new."

P.S. The boys succeeded in "repairing" the vașe and, needless to say, that glue-covered, crooked, cracked vase is among my most treasured possessions!

But I Don't Have It All Together!

Lord, thou wilt ordain peace for us: for thou also hast wrought all our works in us. — Isaiah 26:12, author's emphasis.

WE SAT AROUND THE TABLE, drinking coffee and talking. Suddenly one of the ladies in the group turned to me and said, "Well, after all, *you* have it all together!" Dumfounded, I thought to myself, *Lady if only you knew!*

So with this episode fresh in my mind, it was with reluctance that I walked to the closet and took down my suitcase. On this trip I would be addressing four thousand women on the subject of serenity. As I selected several items of clothing, I was wondering if there were any way I could get out of this commitment. I had no business speaking on a topic I knew so little about and was experiencing so little of in my own life.

Our family had enjoyed a lovely summer vacation in the mountains of North Carolina. After a month of sleeping late, eating well, and breathing cool mountain air, I felt rested and refreshed. But the return two-day trip in the van with nine people had all but destroyed the effects of the vacation.

When we arrived home, we received an emergency telephone call informing us of my grandmother's death, so Stephan and I had repacked and hurriedly returned to North Carolina. After the funeral we called the children only to discover that they were under the threat of a hurricane and we would probably not be able to fly home. Two days and several delays later, we walked in our front door to find that the storm had flooded the living room. We were just recovering from the flood damage when my mother underwent surgery, followed by serious complications. All this on top of getting the children settled in school amid the everyday hassles of managing a large household—and I was supposed to tell four thousand ladies how to experience peace?!

I went into the bathroom where I could be alone and prayed: *Lord, I can't! There is just no way I can go talk to those ladies when I don't know the first thing about serenity!*

Then just as clearly, though not audibly, I heard Him say: *Gigi, you're right. You haven't experienced much serenity in your life lately. But for weeks you have prayed that what you share with those ladies would not be your message, but Mine—and I have everything to share.*

Humbly I said, *Thank You, Lord.* Then I continued to pack. My burden was lifted as I submitted to Him.

> *It is His message—not mine.*
> *It is His will—not mine.*
> *It is His life—not mine.*
> *And that day, during my address to four thousand ladies,*
> *it was His serenity—not mine!*

PASS IT ON . . . "When he giveth quietness, who then can make trouble?" (Job 34:29).

The Plaques

Faint, yet pursuing. — Judges 8:4

THE CHILDREN HAD ALL LEFT for school. With a busy day of writing planned, I wanted to get an early start, so I hurried to clean up the breakfast dishes. I could hear the whir of the washing machine as it spun the first load of wash, and, if I rushed, it would take only a few minutes to straighten the bedrooms. (The cleaning would just have to wait till another day.) I was looking forward to a few hours of productive quiet. I don't work well under pressure, but I don't work at all without it, and I had only a few days left to meet a deadline.

When the phone rang I tried to ignore it. But when it persisted, I picked up the receiver and a cheery voice on the other end asked, "Did I catch you at a bad time?"

Politely I lied: "No, it's fine." I didn't have the heart to refuse a friend who needed some encouragement.

When I finally hung up, I went to put in the second load of wash before heading to my desk. I glanced at my watch and realized that I had only an hour before my kindergartner would be home. I sat down at the desk, prayed, and began to work. The doorbell rang. Oh, no! I had completely forgotten that it was the second Thursday of the month—the day the bug man comes.

Just as he drove away, Jerushah walked in the door. As I fixed her a peanut butter and jelly sandwich, I looked at the calendar. The next day twenty-four fifth-graders would be coming for a swimming party, and then I was expecting twenty for a potluck dinner that same evening. Another week had flown past and I felt as if I hadn't accomplished anything. Panic began to rise. How would I ever finish?

I sank into a chair and buried my face in my hands, exhausted. Too much pressure and tension, complicated by six months of pregnancy, had drained me physically and emotionally. I felt completely frustrated. I wanted to meet the deadline, and yet my daily duties and responsibilities seemed to crowd in. I was tired of all the interruptions and the steady stream of small, insignificant obligations that occupied so much of my time and robbed me of the energy to accomplish what I thought were important goals.

My mind focused on the large wooden plaque which hangs above my mother's kitchen sink:

DIVINE SERVICES CONDUCTED HERE DAILY

Could it be that all these routine, mundane duties were really "divine services"? Was it possible that encouraging a friend, sharing my pool, picking up toys, cleaning and cooking for company, even making peanut butter and jelly sandwiches were of more eternal value than meeting deadlines?

Had I convinced myself that I was doing these "important" things for the Lord, when in reality they were for me and my own ego? Had the temporal once again obscured the eternal? Had I allowed my priorities to become misplaced?

I opened my eyes, and they fell on another plaque, framed in bright yellow and hanging on my own wall:

PRAISE AND PRAY AND PEG AWAY

I had to smile. I knew the Lord was using this method to speak directly to me. His direction and desire for us is not as complicated as we tend to make it. So I again bowed my head and turned over to Him my time and energy, my calendar and my schedule, asking Him for His wisdom and strength in coordinating the details and accepting even the interruptions as from Him. Then I got up, thanking Him and praising Him and proceeding to peg away at the next duty.

As I cleaned the remnants of the peanut butter and jelly sandwich from the table (and the floor) and wiped sticky fingers (and a stickier face), the telephone rang again.

Smiling to myself, I went willingly to answer it, realizing that I was performing a divine service.

(P.S. I met the deadline, too!)

PASS IT ON . . . "And whatsoever ye do, do it heartily, as unto the Lord, and not unto men; knowing that of the Lord ye shall receive the reward" (Col. 3:23-24).

Am I Appetizing?

Be careful how you behave among your unsaved neighbors; for then, even if they are suspicious of you and talk against you, they will end up praising God for your good works when Christ returns. — 1 Peter 2:12 LB

WE TURNED THE KEY and opened the door. The children could not contain their excitement and pushed past us, racing from room to room to explore their new home. Soon the large moving van appeared and backed slowly up the driveway to unload our furniture.

Moving day is a scene that has been repeated many times, for our family has lived in several foreign countries, including France, Switzerland, and Israel, and in many different communities in the United States.

Each time we arrive in a new location, we sense that our neighbors don't know just what to expect. A family with seven children is bad enough, but the fact that I am Billy Graham's daughter and the mother of his grandchildren brings varied reactions. Some are pleased, some are dubious, many are downright intimidated, but all are curious. Will we quote Bible verses all day? Or preface each sentence with "The Bible says"? Will we preach from our back yard, or try other methods to "convert" them? Will we condemn their lifestyle? One neighbor later admitted that he was certain God was trying to "sandwich" him when we bought the house next door! Another came to our door and found my hair in rollers. "Oh!" he exclaimed. "You wear rollers?" I guess he thought an angel arranged my hair during the night.

But they soon learn that rollers are more in vogue in our house than halos, that we mow our lawn, shop for groceries, and pay our bills like everyone else. They discover that our children argue, that I frequently scream at them to quit, that we are, in short, far from perfect—very normal, ordinary people. So they begin to relax. But I do take my Christian witness seriously, and I am always conscious of the fact that I represent the Lord Jesus.

As a child I awoke one morning and dragged myself down

the stairs to breakfast. Mother had overslept, so she had hurriedly put on her robe, then grabbed Franklin out of his crib without bothering to comb her hair or change his diaper. When I arrived in the kitchen, she was standing over the stove frying bacon, Franklin was banging on his high chair, Bunny was talking a blue streak, and Anne was silently picking at her plate. After looking around, I threw down my fork and said, "Mama, between looking at you, smelling Franklin, and listening to Bunny, I'm just not hungry!"

Now I take a critical look at our family and our lifestyle. Are we appetizing? I examine myself, my attitude toward the children, how I answer the door or the telephone, how I react when someone pushes ahead of me in line at the grocery store, how I dress, how I behave when I think no one recognizes me. Would I want *me* for a neighbor?

Do I practice my Christianity in practical ways? Do others see Jesus in me? Do they observe patience and kindness? Am I approachable, accessible, available? When guests walk into my home, do they feel welcome? Do they feel the presence of the Lord? Are those who live around us and come in contact with us attracted to Him? Or are they just not hungry?

PASS IT ON . . . It has been said that you may well doubt the reality of your Christian experience if your life does not demand an explanation. May our lives cause others to hunger and thirst for righteousness.

My Heart Is Too Small

I will run the way of thy commandments, when thou shalt enlarge my heart. — Psalm 119:32

IT WAS EARLY MORNING and I had a busy schedule planned. Suddenly I heard a knock at the front door. When I opened it, I groaned inwardly. There stood a friend with a tendency to create problems for herself, and she needed a sounding board. I sighed and invited her to come in.

Some time later, as we sat by the open fire, drinking coffee and watching the snowflakes swirl outside the window, she poured out her heart. I was stunned, unable to believe what I was hearing. This woman whom I had housed, fed, and helped on numerous occasions was reciting a litany of complaints and resentments toward me that wounded and confused me. By the time she left, I was bewildered and deeply hurt.

I stumbled through the rest of my day, automatically preparing dinner, carrying on conversations, and putting the children to bed. I couldn't sleep that night and lay in bed, allowing the disappointment and hurt to fester into bitterness. What had given her the right to speak to me as she had—to expect so much from me? It seemed that the more I gave, the more she expected and the less she appreciated. Why was she so defensive, so thoughtless?

In the following days my hurt feelings grew into what could only be called anger, but I called it "righteous indignation." Since it was painful to be around my friend, I tried to avoid her and gradually built a protective wall about myself. The weeks lengthened into months and I was still far from attempting to understand or to remedy the situation. The more I thought about her unjust accusations, the more resentful I felt.

But the Lord has marvelous ways of gently rebuking us when we are not walking worthy of Him. And it wasn't long before He made me aware that my attitude was anything but Christlike.

One of my younger children was acting especially cantankerous one day. He was disobedient, sassy, rude, obstinate—you name it. He blamed everyone in the family for making his life miserable. Finally, hoping to get to the bottom of things, we sat him down and asked him why his attitude was so awful.

"Well," he replied, "I guess it's because my heart is too small."

Could this be my problem, too? Was my heart so narrow, so limited, so self-centered that I had failed to explore the reasons behind my friend's actions? Had I allowed my injured ego to close the door to the very part of me the Lord wanted to use in this woman's life? Was I suffering from a shriveled heart?

To my shame I thought of the times the Lord had graciously looked beyond my faults, which often camouflaged my own hidden needs. Instead of condemning me along with my failures, He had gone right to the point of the need and touched it with His healing love. God is love and love is kind, not touchy; it does not hold grudges and hardly notices when others do it wrong. (See 1 Cor. 13 LB.) Love always takes a second look!

Suddenly I knew that the Lord expected me to deal with my friend as He always deals with me—gently, lovingly, fully forgiving. So I began to look beyond her irritating flaws and hurtful words and discovered insecurity, low self-esteem, envy, loneliness, and other difficulties she was bravely trying to cope with.

I asked the Lord to forgive my attitude and to give me compassion, wisdom, understanding, and largeness of heart (1 Kings 4:29) so that I could begin to share not only *her* burdens (Col. 6:2), but those of the many others whose paths cross mine.

PASS IT ON . . . "It is only with the heart that one sees rightly."

Fruitful Frustration

When thou passeth through the waters, I will be with thee. — Isaiah
43:2

EACH YEAR, AS SCHOOL NEARS an end and summer
survival begins, I face the months ahead with mixed emotions. I
enjoy being with the children and having a more relaxed
schedule. But I dread: a permanently disorderly house; the
multiple arguments that require me, the resident judge, to
settle; the wet towels and paper cups that seem to sprout up all
over the house and yard; the thousands of times I have to
scream, "Close the door! The air conditioner is on and we aren't
cooling all of Coral Springs!"

It is the same frustrating feeling I experience when the dishes
have just been put away and everyone comes trooping into the
kitchen—hungry again! So for three months of the year, I try to
find creative ways of turning my frustrations into fruitfulness.

It was on one of these days that I came across a delightful
little verse tucked away in Joshua: "For the Jordan [River]
overfloweth all his banks all the time of harvest" (3:15). What
comfort and strength I received from that verse. Satan may
send flooding and overflowing difficulties into our lives to
discourage and defeat us, but the Lord can use those very same
elements to produce a harvest!

The Nile Delta is considered to be one of the most fertile areas
of the world. Since the year 3600 B.C. until 1968, when the
Aswan High Dam was built to control irrigation, the Nile
flooded its banks each year—a cause for great celebration and
rejoicing. The anticipated harvest was of much more value and
significance than the temporary inconvenience.

So it is in our lives. The flooding is used to make the soil of
our lives fertile, tillable, and fruitful. Though we may be
unaware, the Lord is using the difficulties, the overwhelming
problems, the unexpected to reap a harvest for His glory. He is
turning our frustrations into fruitfulness.

The little things that bug me,
resentments deep within;
the things I ought to do, undone
the irritations one by one
till nerves stretch screaming-thin
and bare for all the world to see—
which needs His touch to make it whole
the most, my body or my soul?

I pray—but nothing comes out right,
my thoughts go flying everywhere;
my attitudes are all confused,
I hate myself—I am not used
to hands all clenched, not clasped, in prayer,
and heart too leaden to take flight;
which, oh, which, needs to be whole
the most, my body or my soul?

I cannot read. I cannot pray.
I cannot even think.
Where to from here? and how get there
with only darkness everywhere?
I ought to rise and only sink. . .
and feel His arms, and hear Him say,
"I love you.". . .It was all my soul
or body needed to be whole.
                        — Ruth Bell Graham*

PASS IT ON . . . If your life is overflowing with difficulties, remember that "faith can read love in God's heart even when His face frowns." —James Renwick

*From *Sitting by My Laughing Fire* by Ruth Bell Graham, copyright © 1977 by Ruth Bell Graham; used by permission of Word Books, Publisher, Waco, Texas 76796.

Help, Lord! I Need Strength!

For when I am weak, then I am strong—the less I have, the more I depend on him. — *2 Corinthians 12:10 NIV*

THE GIANT PLANE LIFTED off the ground, making the familiar landmarks visible for only a few moments before its nose pierced the billowy white clouds and leveled off in the clear blue atmosphere. Outside my window, all was quiet and calm and peaceful—so unlike the way I felt inside.

Worn out in both body and spirit, I was grateful that no one was sitting in the seat beside me. I needed this time to be alone. Closing my eyes, I leaned back against the seat, hoping for a bit of much-needed rest. But my mind continued to whirl like the fast, cheap thrill rides at the carnival. Flying high above the earth that day, I wished with David that these powerful wings would take me away where I could be at rest. (See Ps. 55:6.)

With my eyes still closed, I listened to the drone of the powerful engines, thinking about another weary woman who, some years before, had discovered her Source of strength. Mrs. Jonathan Goforth had many pressures and responsibilities as a busy wife, mother, and missionary to China. One day, finding herself overburdened and her strength insufficient, she turned to the Scriptures. She was surprised and overjoyed to find that even the weakest may fulfill the conditions for receiving strength outlined there:

1. *Weakness:* 2 Corinthians 12:9, 10
2. *No Might:* Isaiah 40:29
3. *Sitting Still:* Isaiah 30:7
4. *Waiting on God:* Isaiah 40:31
5. *Quietness:* Isaiah 30:15
6. *Confidence:* Isaiah 30:15
7. *Joy in the Lord:* Nehemiah 8:10
8. *Poor:* Isaiah 25:4
9. *Needy:* Isaiah 25:4
10. *Abiding In Christ:* Philippians 4:13

As I sat there, thinking and silently praying, I realized I had only fulfilled a couple of these conditions. I had not been sitting still and waiting, but running here and there, trusting in myself instead of placing my confidence in Him. I had not been waiting on the Lord in an atmosphere of quietness, but in a state of tension and anxiety until, once again, I had all but lost the joy of the Lord.

As the plane began its descent, I felt strangely warmed and renewed. My inner spirit began to sing: "Blessed be the Lord, because he hath heard the voice of my supplications. The Lord is my strength . . . my heart trusted IN HIM, and I am helped: therefore my heart greatly rejoiceth; and with my song will I praise him" (Ps. 28:6-7).

PASS IT ON . . . When our strength is depleted, we can simply turn to Him who is an inexhaustible source of strength, and exchange our insufficiency for His all-sufficiency.

The Valley

But the land, whither ye go to possess it, is a land of hills and valleys.
— Deuteronomy 11:11

STEPHAN AND I HAD FINISHED our shopping and had stopped for tea at Chez Manuel on La Place St. Francois. It was getting late, and we would have to hurry if we were to arrive at the chalet in time for supper. However, when we left the city of Lausanne, we chose the small winding road that hugged the edge of Lac Leman instead of the freeway, sacrificing time for beauty.

The afternoon sun sparkled on the lake dotted with small sailboats, whose occupants were taking advantage of the warm days of late summer. The majestic mountain peaks were reflected in its deep blue stillness, and the large paddle boat, crowded with tourists, passed in elegant silence, broken only by the shrill whistle as it approached the next stop. The hills climbed sharply to our left, where many centuries of hard work had formed terrace upon terrace of neat vineyards. The vines were now laden with fruit soon to be gathered by the men and women who inhabited the ancient villages nestled on the hillsides overlooking the lake.

We drove through Vevey, then Montreux, where we had been married in the seventeenth-century church twenty years earlier. We passed the historic castle of Chillon, poised on the water's edge. Then, leaving the lake behind us, we entered the Rhone Valley where the soil is rich and black. Here, there were not only vineyards, but orchards of apples and lush peaches, and fertile fields yielding fruits and vegetables of every kind.

It wasn't long before we left the main highway and started up the steep, narrow, alpine road that would take us home to our village. We were forced to slow down every few minutes because of the long, hairpin curves snaking around the sides of the mountain and carrying us up and away from the valley floor. No longer did we see vineyards or orchards or fertile fields—only a small vegetable patch or flower garden here and there, and fields of hay, dotted with farmers cutting rhythmically with their long-handled scythes. Their wives, heads wrapped in brightly colored kerchiefs, raked alongside them.

We continued climbing, passing the old church of Huemoz where Stephan had been baptized as a child. We drove through our village, the steep road taking us past the chalet with dark green shutters where he had been born, higher and higher, until we reached our own chalet, clinging to the side of the mountain and nestled among the evergreen trees.

We were met enthusiastically by the children, all vying for attention and the candies they knew would be in our pockets.

Soon we sat down to a meal of Gruyere cheese, sausage, and thick Swiss bread. After supper I bathed the children and tucked them into bed. Then, going downstairs where all was quiet, I put water on for tea and lit the fire.

I sat gazing out over the valley below where we had passed only a short time before. Often it is obscured by clouds and fog, but tonight the air was crisp and clear and the light from the full moon rising over the ridge bathed it in a soft glow. I remembered the clusters of ripening fruit, the orchards and fields almost ready for harvest. Then I looked past the valley to the French Alps beyond. They were magnificent. I could even glimpse Mont Blanc, the highest peak in all of Western Europe. Most of these mountains are snow-covered year-round, and I never tire of their awesome beauty.

Sipping my tea and watching the moon caress each peak as it rose higher and higher into the midnight sky, I thought of the mountains surrounding us, their steep ridges climaxing into sharp peaks just behind our chalet. They, too, were splendid, but with the exception of a few flowers and evergreen trees, quite barren and desolate. I thought of my life and how similar it is to these surroundings—its ups and downs, its mountains and valleys. I have always dreaded the valley times, finding clouds and rain disagreeable and much preferring the warmth and brightness of the sun. I have striven for the mountaintop experiences, seeking to avoid the dense fog of struggle and pain.

The fire cast a cozy glow. As I finished my tea, I realized that, although I had found exhilaration and excitement on the mountaintops, it was in the valleys that I had experienced real growth. It was there that the Lord had plowed, planted, pruned, and reaped a harvest in my life.

I sighed. In my spiritual selfishness, I loved the mountains, but the true test comes when we come down from the mountains. I longed to grow in Him and to bear fruit for His glory. So I bowed my head, thanking Him for mountain splendor, but also thanking Him for the valleys, willing now to accept them, submitting to the rain and fog, the plowing and the pruning, knowing that He who plants the seed and tills the soil will bring forth fruit.

PASS IT ON . . . We see and experience the glory of God on the mountaintops, but we live it out in the valleys.

"Every valley shall be exalted, and every mountain and hill shall be made low. . . .and the glory of the Lord shall be revealed" (Isa. 40:4-5).

I LEAVE YOU...FOR NOW

A sudden shiver brought me back to the present. Many years had come and gone in my memory as I sat huddled on the hearth. Now all that was left of the fire were a few softly glowing embers buried beneath the grate.

I thanked the Lord for this time of remembering and thought how vital and important and precious it was. No wonder He had told the children of Israel to "remember the days of old"; to remember His commandments (Num. 15:39-40); to remember how He had delivered them (Deut. 15:15) and led them (Deut. 8:2); to remember to trust Him and not to be afraid (Deut. 7:18); to remember "His wonderful works which were made to be remembered" (Ps. 111:4).

I thought how my faith and trust in Almighty God had been established and grounded through hearing repeatedly the stories of God's faithfulness through the years. I thought of all that I had experienced in my own life and of all that I wanted to pass on to my children in order to build up their faith, and resolved to remind them more often of all He has done for us.

Perhaps we could begin some traditions of our own—keeping a list of answers to prayer, or a scrapbook of God's goodness. The children had enjoyed thumbing through their grandparents' old photograph albums—laughing at pictures of me when I was a child, meeting great-great-grandparents for the first time, reliving happy moments. It occurred to me that we could also build a spiritual scrapbook—sharing memories of spiritual victories stored in our minds.

I readjusted the warm mohair shawl around my shoulders and walked slowly to the window. All was silent. The snow had stopped, covering the world outside the window in a soft white blanket. The stars shone brightly in the dark clear sky. Tomorrow promised to be a glorious day.

And so, I leave you for now with the challenge to pass it on and "tell to the generation to come the praises of the Lord, and His strength and how wondrous works that He has done. That the generation to come might know, even the children yet to be born, that they may arise and tell them to their children, that they should put their confidence in God, and not forget the works of God, but keep His commandments" (Ps. 78:4, 6, 7 NASB).

IN APPRECIATION

To Stephan, whose love, encouragement, and tender care kept
  me going
To Berdjette, my daughter who faithfully and with love typed
  and retyped this manuscript
To Sarah, who sweetly and unselfishly relieved me of many of
  my household responsibilities so that I would be free to write
To Ann, who challenged me as both editor and friend
To my family, who put up with me
And to all the Zondervan family who made it possible
I simply and lovingly say, "Thank you."

ACKNOWLEGMENTS

Scripture quotations are from the King James Version unless otherwise designated. Modern translations used are:

The Amplified Bible, Old Testament. Copyright © 1962, 1964 by the Zondervan Publishing House. Used by permission. (*Amplified*)

The Good News Bible, the Bible in Today's English Version. Old Testament: Copyright © American Bible Society, 1976; New Testament: Copyright © American Bible Society 1966, 1971, 1976. Used by permission. (TEV)

The Living Bible, paraphrased, Copyright © Tyndale House Publishers, Wheaton, Illinois, 1971. Used by permission. (LB)

The New American Standard Bible. Copyright © The Lockman Foundation, 1960, 1962, 1963, 1968, 1971, 1972, 1973, 1975, 1977. Used by permission. (NASB)

The New English Bible, Copyright © The Delegates of the Oxford University Press and the Syndics of the Cambridge University Press, 1961, 1970. Reprinted by permission. (NEB)

THE HOLY BIBLE: NEW INTERNATIONAL VERSION. Copyright © 1978 by the International Bible Society. Used by permission of Zondervan Bible Publishers. (NIV)

The New Testament in Modern English, Revised Edition, by J. B. Phillips, copyright © J. B. Phillips 1958, 1960, 1972. Reprinted by permission of Macmillan Publishing Company, Inc. (*Phillips*)